AF541500

國家圖書館出版社

[illegible]

[illegible] 010-66114536 [illegible]
網　　址 http://www.[illegible]
排　　版 北京[illegible]章文化[illegible]公司
印　　裝 北京[illegible]藝齋古籍[illegible]有限責任公司
版次印次 2022年12月第1版　2022年12月第1次印刷

開　　本 [illegible]
印　　張 [illegible]
字　　數 [illegible]千字
書　　號 ISBN 978-7-5013-[illegible]
定　　價 200.00圓

'A powerful book, much needed in a time when the multiculturalism of India is under threat. Indian thoughts and ways of life are not just brahminical, pseudo-spiritual, inward-looking, life-denying, patriarchal and unequal—labels that dominate the narrative now. There have been powerful subaltern streams of thought that have risen from this soil to challenge oppressive hegemonies in all eras. This book is a reminder of that continuing rebellion. Lucidly written and thought provoking, *Antigod's Own Country* helps us understand that every god needs an antigod'

Anand Neelakantan, author, *Asura: Tale of the Vanquished*

'Sakthidharan's reconfiguration of the stories that dominate the Malayali imagination reminds us that myths are born and flourish in historical time. They reflect and amplify the political and social exigencies that frame them. If we listen to myths fully, we realise that instead of establishing cultural hegemony, they are often subversive and contrary'

Arshia Sattar, translator, *Valmiki's Ramayana*

'Piercing in its scrutiny of assumed histories, and provocative in challenging narrative hegemonies, *Antigod's Own Country* is an instructive overview of Kerala's religious and cultural heterogeneity, highlighting the traditions of the marginalised and unremembered to celebrate the land of Maveli'

Manu S. Pillai, author, *Rebel Sultans*

'Saktidharan's well-researched and erudite book blends mythology and history, economics and literature, to investigate the belief systems that shape the complex social fabric of Kerala. By looking at the interpretations of the myths of Maveli and Vamana, Ayyappa, and syncretic folk traditions, *Antigod's Own Country* challenges and subverts the hegemonic narrative of Hinduism and caste. It forces us to rethink categories of deva and asura, good and evil, right and wrong. This is essential reading for every Indian'

Samhita Arni, author, *Sita's Ramayana*

Antigod's Own Country
A Short History of Brahminical Colonisation of Kerala

First published on Onam, 1 September 2019. Reprinted 2024

ISBN 9788189059941

Navayana Publishing Pvt Ltd
155 2nd Floor
Shahpur Jat, New Delhi 110049
navayana.org

Typeset by Birendra in Garamond

Printed by Sanjiv Palliwal, New Delhi

Distributed in South Asia by HarperCollins India

Subscribe to updates at navayana.org/subscribe

ANTIGOD'S OWN COUNTRY

A SHORT HISTORY OF BRAHMINICAL COLONISATION OF KERALA

A.V. Sakthidharan

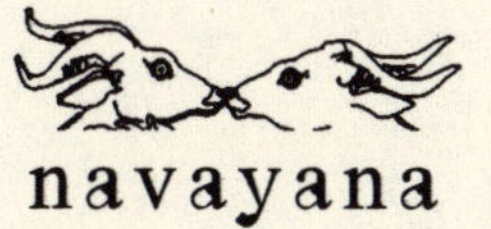

navayana

A.V. Sakthidharan has worked as a journalist for close to four decades and retired from *The Hindustan Times* in Delhi as Assistant Editor in 2006. This is his first book.

In memory of my life partner Devaky
who did not live to see this book

Contents

Introduction

THE STORY told is this: fifth century BCE saw the migration of large swathes of people from Eastern Europe further eastwards. These travellers, branching out into Iran and India, settled down in new territories, birthing new cultures. When one imagines this event, a famished caravan looking for a better life comes to mind. No doubt the process was slower and less intentional; the aspirations of the migrants in their gradual movement is difficult to surmise. It is equally hard to ascertain their colonial aspirations; but colonise they did, and the reverberations of this colonisation are felt to this day.

In this migration one sees the birth of what we call today Hinduism. The Vedas, spiritual ruminations of the yajna-obsessed Aryan migrants to India, formed the base of Hinduism though the religion was not known by that moniker until the eighth century CE. 'Hindu' was a portmanteau used by the Turks and the Arabs for the people living beyond the Indus. The religion does not have any historical founder, prophet or a definitive holy book as in the case of Semitic religions. Gods worshipped in the Vedic age—Indra, Agni, Yama, Varuna—later yielded place to Ganesha, Rama, Krishna, and so on. Followers of shramanic faiths who challenged the Vedas were condemned as asuras, rakshasas and rakshasis. The puranas, which burgeoned between 400 and 1400 CE, marked the triumph of brahminism over shramanism. In the hands of the authors of the puranas, the religious faith of the Dharmashastras and the Smritis underwent a gradual transformation and thus was born what is known as puranic Hinduism. The Bhagavad Gita, another important religious text, was an interpolation in the Mahabharata written between the second and the fourth century CE; Mahabharata's regional language versions largely ignored the Gita, in which Krishna, among other things, defends chaturvarnya and patriarchy. From the seventh century onwards, starting with Tamil and spreading to Kannada, Marathi and various registers of what's come to be called Hindi by the sixteenth century, the so-called bhakti movement threw up a host of poets born into the working castes, who used a proletarian language, and challenged the tenets of brahminism. Ultimately the puranic religion of the Aryans sought to appropriate all these challenges, and backed by the state, it triumphed and qualified for the 'mainstream' label. Its latest iteration are the godmen and godwomen of the twentieth century.

Hinduism had no compunctions in borrowing gods from the pre-Aryan tribal culture. Vishnu, a minor Vedic deity compared to Agni and Indra, later grew into a more important god when the sage Narayana merged with a group of deified clan heroes. Totemic gods like the primeval fish, the toad and the boar—common to many adivasi creation and evolution myths—graduated into incarnations of Vishnu. Hinduism continues to draw heavily from local faith systems: there were reports of attempts in Maharashtra to divest some Sufi shrines of their Islamic identity for inclusion in the Hindu pantheon. Small wonder, as the religion has even co-opted the Buddha, who was no believer in god, into its fold as the ninth incarnation of Vishnu.

The dominant brahminical account of Indian culture and history was reinforced by the colonial masters and the European Orientalists who manufactured a spiritual India and reduced the knowledge system of the land to the Vedas, Upanishads, puranas and the Bhagavad Gita. Secular tomes in the fields of atheist thought, Ayurveda and mathematics and works like the *Kamasutra* were cleverly given the short shrift. America-born Col Henry Steel Olcott (1832–1907), one of the founders of the Theosophical Society in Madras, regarded the Aryans as the ancestors of the Hindus and the progenitors of European civilisation. Max Mueller ignored the role of Islamic culture in India and described the Muslim rule as tyrannical. Under Mahatma Gandhi's leadership the Congress, which was originally a platform of well-heeled professionals, was transformed into a movement of the masses. However, both Gandhi and the avowed non-believer, Nehru, identified the religion with the nation. Hinduism became a powerful symbol of elite nationalism and there have been persistent efforts to manufacture a monolithic religious system for India.

Alongside the rise of such religious supremacists, there also emerged antagonistic perspectives. B.R. Ambedkar denied Hinduism the very status of a religion; he called it a mere collection of castes. Sree Narayana Guru (1855–1928), who fought against brahminism in Kerala, was also convinced that there can be no such thing as a Hindu religion. Some believe that there are several 'Hindu religions'. Dalits, tribals and other subaltern groups, who have no inhibitions about offering meat and liquor to goddesses and spirits during puja, have the condescending term 'folk Hinduism' thrust upon them by inclusion-minded folks attempting to standardise a multiplicity of practises.

In India the prevailing tendency is to categorise every faith that is not Christianity, Islam or Sikhism as Hinduism. A more nuanced approach tends to view not just Buddhism and Jainism, but also Vaishnavism, Saivism and Shaktism as autonomous religions. Take the Lingayats of Karnataka. Although they worship Siva, their religious position has been contested as non-Hindu. Founded in the twelfth century by the social reformer, Basaveshwara, Vedic rituals have no place in the Lingayat faith. Even the use of Sanskrit in rituals was abandoned in favour of Kannada. Lingayatism was also opposed to caste distinctions. The monotheistic faith found favour from a large representation of subaltern communities—barbers, peasants, washermen, shepherds, sex workers—besides upper-class scholars, and provided inspiration to dalit movements in the region.

Hinduism is often described as a mosaic of cultures. Such a description leaves a number of independent syncretic cults at the mercy of an all-embracing faith system and its muscular storm-troopers. Various regions in India, rather sub-nations, have nurtured their own independent spiritual and religious cultures which are separate from brahminical Hinduism of the Aryavrata kind. The Kali worship of Bengal, Odisha's Jagannath cult and the tribal cultures of the North East are some examples. Puri's famous Jagannath temple has had an undeniable tribal character: during the famous rath yatra, Jagannath's chariot stops at his shrine to pay respects to Bhakta Salabega, an ardent Muslim devotee who is credited with a number of poems in praise of the deity. Yet the Jagannath temple is thought of as Hindu.

This is part of a long history of Aryan–brahmin hegemony that has relentlessly appropriated Dravidian 'Hinduism' after stripping it of its egalitarian characteristics. Even in the modern age, elite purveyors of culture betray an anti-Dravidian, anti-lower caste and anti-Muslim bias. The very idea of a geographic entity called India stems from the puranic concept of Bharatvarsha, which has its origins in the works of ancient astronomers like Varahamihira and Bhaskaracharya. This conception excludes vast regions of the now-consolidated India, especially its southern parts. For us, such an exclusion is helpful: we can look at the remnants of vanquished ancient cultures which were forcefully erased, and eke out a past preserved in mythology as hints at a more egalitarian structure of society. This book foregrounds the surviving vibrant religious cultures, which are subaltern, subnational and subversive, differing in form and content from the so-called mainstream Hinduism. We set our sights on the particular case of Kerala, whose exclusion from several currents of mainstream Hinduism now seems inevitable.

Kerala is a narrow strip of land nestled in the lush and fragile ecology of the Western Ghats in the southwest corner of the Indian subcontinent. Neighboured by Karnataka and Tamil Nadu to the east, its coast is perpetually lapped by the Arabian Sea. Forty-four rivers traverse through the province of 38,855 square kilometres. Kerala is one of the smallest units in the federation of sub-nations that is India.

History and material conditions have a crucial role in shaping the culture and religious beliefs of every land. Tamizhakam which enveloped Kerala was never ruled by imperial dynasties like the Mauryas or the Guptas, Pathans or Mughals. Ambitious and expansionist though he was, even Aurangzeb could push the borders of the Mughal empire only as far as Tamizhakam. Kerala being one of India's gateways, it maintained contact with several countries through flourishing trade relations. Vessels from Arabia, Egypt, Rome and Greece were a frequent sight in the major port of Muziris, present-day Kodungallur, in central

Kerala. Later, Portuguese traders came seeking spices, followed by the Dutch and finally the British.

Naturally there was a composite influence on the way of life in this southern state. Take for example Islam: the distinct practices of Muslims in this province reflects the Mappilas' integration with local culture and their isolation from their North Indian co-religionists. The construction of mosques follows a decidedly local architectural motif. A number of Muslim festivals, including the 'nerchas' and the Chandanakkudam festival at Beemappalli have indigenous roots. There is even a Mappila Ramayanam in Malayalam. As for the Christians, who form roughly twenty per cent of the population, their cultural, social, political and economic life in the state is an amalgam of Christian values and Indic rituals. Malayali Christians have the bragging rights of being some of the oldest converts to the religion in the world. St Thomas, one of the twelve apostles of Jesus, is believed to have landed in Muziris in 52 CE, founded churches, preached gospels and converted a large contingent of locals, including a ruler. The Christians have been so comfortably embedded in the local culture that they even practise the caste system without compunction. The borderline between one religion and another is thus quite thin in Kerala. Non-theistic faiths like Buddhism and Jainism thrived here for long, exerting a lasting influence on Malayali culture.

Thanks to these material factors, Kerala differs from the rest of the country in history and culture, and as she grows up the Malayali learns to see her state as much more than a part of India. This province has more in common with Buddhist Sri Lanka than other parts of India. It is not surprising that Kerala boasts of quite a few non-Aryan religious and cultural icons.

Antigod's Own Country is a narrative which straddles history and mythology: the book unapologetically blends and moves from one to the other. At the risk of over-estimating the value of mythology, its importance lies in how it reveals the structural assumptions and the unspoken bonds of the society which creates it. A large part of Indian history vis-à-vis its mythology is assumed to be the landscape of upper-caste and Aryan subjects. This book is an attempt to reclaim mythology from such a matrix of power and make visible the multiple practices that have for years withstood brahminical pressures and continue to face attempts of appropriation. We begin with the Vamana myth, which together with the fib about Parashurama, another Vishnu avatar, retrieving land from the sea and gifting it to the brahmins, signals the arrival of brahminism in Kerala in the Mauryan era and its reception with boundless land gifts from local rulers.

Myths are powerful carriers of the subversive feelings, protests against injustice and aspirational conjectures of subjugated peoples. The story goes that there was neither inequality nor malfeasance of any kind during the rule of Maveli, before his kingdom was gobbled up by Vamana, a brahmin avatar of Lord Vishnu. Maveli's distraught consort Vindhyawali and son Banasura strongly resented the injustice done to the asura king. The asuras prepared for war against the invader but were dissuaded by Maveli from shedding blood. The love for Maveli among his subjects was such that they stretched the story creatively: folklore has it that they pleaded with the ousted ruler to visit them every year. The diminutive Vamana, upon realising that the allegiance of those he had conquered couldn't be easily swayed, decided not to oppose this request. So, come the month of Chingam, on the colourful day of Thiruvonam, this icon of the non-Aryan past 'returns' to the Malayali mindscape to a hero's welcome.

Here lies the politics of Onam and the Maveli myth. The invitation from the people to Maveli was a politically and ideologically loaded statement, a creative response to an unpardonable act of injustice done to a just ruler. The people were refusing to accept the hegemony of the invader. There are a number of songs which look back nostalgically to the halcyon days of Maveli's rule which ended with the arrival of the gods. The bulk of these have been authored by members of the panan and parayan communities, dalits both.

Pierre Bourdieu conceptualises cultural capital as a form of power beyond the economic form, exercised through various non-economic means. The arrival of brahminism reversed all mechanisms of cultural production of the original inhabitants: those parts of their mythology which held the pride of place were made into the antagonistic principle in the Hindu landscape. This robbed subaltern castes of their accumulated cultural capital, immediately relegating them to the bottom of the new hierarchy. The Tamil-origin god Murugan was one of the first folk gods to be Sanskritised. When the dalit gods were converted to Hinduism, the element of resistance in them faded away. In response to the injustices of brahminical theology and sociality, egalitarian faiths like Buddhism, Jainism and Ajivika developed; to preserve itself, brahminism penetrated into the popular tribal cults. This subsumption happened on both material and psychic levels: materially, the Aryans controlled the economic lives of the old inhabitants, a control which was established through Vamanic force and deceit; psychically, this material proximity and power was exerted to create a social hierarchy in favour of a new order. Witness in the following pages the egalitarian Ayyappa with his Muslim and Christian companions, Mutthappa with an impure dog by his seat, some of the teyyams, goddesses in the kavus, non-vegetarian deities, even the anti-hero of the Mahabharata, Suyodhana, in southern Kerala. This continuity of an older order is a story of a sustained resistance that colours the fabric of Kerala.

The glorification of the asura ruler Mahabali disrupts the decades-long attempt of the Sangh parivar—the cluster of hindutva organisations that are affiliated to the Rashtriya Swayamsevak Sangh—to imprison Kerala within the walls of a fictional Hindu monolith, and their hopes, like that of their predecessors, to sell off an entire society to a crony clutch of billionaires and trillionaires. In this vein, on the eve of Onam in 2016, Amit Shah, then president of the Bharatiya Janata Party (BJP), extended 'Vamana Jayanti' greetings to the people of Kerala. Shah had reason enough to put the myth on its head. Inevitably, the BJP chief faced furious criticism.

The memory of a time when everyone lived happily can be said to have prepared the ground for a series of protest and resistance movements against inequalities and other forms of injustice. It was so that Pottan Teyyam took on Adi Sankara on the question of untouchability and unapproachability; in more modern times, subjugated castes built an ideological apparatus by throwing up a bevy of creative writers and radical intellectuals who questioned the caste system in their own ways. Literature, political fora, conversion and re-reading of religious works were used in shaping an egalitarian ideological apparatus that spawned a new consciousness among the marginalised, and challenged the iniquitous status quo. Potheri Kunhambu's novel *Saraswativijayam* (1892) focused on the need for dalits to receive an English education as a means of social progress, while his *Ramayanasarashodhana*, which appeared in 1893, was a frontal attack on brahmin oppression. Ayyankali (1863–1941) founded the Sadhu Jana Paripalana Sangham in 1907 and confronted upper caste tyranny. Defying an upper caste diktat, the feisty champion of dalit rights rode a decorated bullock cart on a public road. His attempts at getting a pulaya girl into a government school saw the upper castes burn down the entire building. Despite being unlettered, Ayyankali worked tirelessly to secure educational rights for dalits. 'If our children are not allowed to attend classes, weeds will grow in your fields,' he thundered, and successfully led an agricultural workers' strike in the year 1907, well before the birth of the All-India Trade Union Congress in 1920.

Narayana Guru, who coined the slogan 'One god, one religion, one caste for mankind', hit at the very underbelly of sanctimonious brahminism by consecrating a Siva idol in a would-be temple. When the brahmins questioned the right of an ezhavan to perform the consecration, the savant snapped back famously that he had installed an ezhava Siva. Did the scriptures proscribe the installation of an ezhava Siva by a non-brahmin? In an act of protest against caste tyranny, Narayana Guru's disciples Sahodaran Ayyappan and P. Palpu embraced Buddhism. Poykayil Appachan embraced Christianity but soon discovered with dismay that caste prejudices followed him to the supposedly egalitarian faith too. When Appachan found that the Bible could play no emancipatory role in the life of dalit converts to Christianity, he burnt the holy book at a public meeting and many in the audience followed suit. He survived several attempts on his life by 'upper caste Christians'.

Thus, the privileged castes faced regular and truculent challenges in this southern state long before North India saw the birth of combative anti-brahmin campaigns. Radical namboodiri youth of the day like V.T. Raman Bhattathiripad and E.M.S. Namboodiripad, who fought the deep patriarchal philistinism in their community, and the militant Left, which was voted to office in the state in 1957, drew inspiration from the life and ideas of the leaders of the subaltern movements.

Despite all this, the state remains caught in a past where the dominant social forces oppress dalits and adivasis, and deny them equal rights and privileges. The bureaucracy and political parties are the new purveyors of caste prejudices. The official car used by a retiring dalit bureaucrat is 'purified' before it is given to his savarna successor; a talented percussion artist is excluded from a team playing 'panchavadyam', an ensemble of five instruments, in the Guruvayur temple because he belongs to a 'low caste'; non-dalit auto-rickshaw drivers in a village burn a pulaya woman's vehicle because she chooses to make a living by storming a male bastion. The police force lends a helping hand in maintaining this dynamic. In spite of the much-trumpeted high female literacy rate and sex ratio, patriarchy is deeply entrenched in Kerala society. Sexual violence against women is rampant.

This slim volume was originally intended to be a Maveli Reader. But the sheer number of rebellious figures meant that the ambit of *Antigod's Own Country* was extended to examine all these variant themes. The mythological asura king who ruled over the three worlds in Tretayuga makes space for his kin and ideological non-asura cousins. The first chapter covers the Onam festival, when Malayalis extend a hearty welcome to Maveli, its hijack by the market, the story of Vamana and the ramifications of the myth. The second chapter looks at the Marxist perception of the utopian Maveli regime as primitive communism and how this non-antagonistic mode of production yielded place to an antagonistic mode: landlordism sprang from the brahmins' near-total control over land and spiritual life and the caste system. The third chapter dwells at some length on the persona of Maveli and covers the enviable position he occupies on the literary-academic firmament. The next chapter is on the asura community to which Maveli belonged and its icons like Ravana and Mahishasura. Chapter 5 focuses on the assorted gods and goddesses worshipped in Kerala, most of them strangers to brahminical Hinduism. The Buddhist roots of Onam and the influence of rational shramana faiths in this region are put under the scanner in the sixth chapter. The book concludes with a short account of recent developments and the relentless campaigns to Hinduise Mavelinadu, where the logic of a monolithic pan-Indian Hindu culture and hindutva nationalism are entirely antithetical to its societal character.

1

A Festival of Memory

MAVELI or Mahabali, or just Bali for some, was the great-grandson of the other great asura Hiranyakashipu, and is said to have ruled the three worlds, earth, heaven and the underworld, aeons ago in Tretayuga. He ascended to the throne in a time of fierce contest between the suras and the asuras. With his reputation as a just ruler and a fierce warrior on the rise, the suras sat conspiring in their displeasure. Maveli had already secured many boons to become invincible and the jealous gods in their impotence took up deceitful means to bring down the benevolent king. In a false gesture of peace, they requested Maveli to help them churn the celestial ocean in order to obtain Indra's treasure that had fallen into its depths. In reality, they were trying to create the nectar of immortality for use in their war with the asuras. Only Maveli was skilled enough to churn an entire ocean. He agreed readily in the hope of ending the ancient strife between their clans. But when the trickery of the gods was found, war broke out. The asuras stormed the celestial realm and gained control over the entire universe. In defeating Indra, Maveli is said to have ushered in a utopian age of peace and prosperity. One doesn't get this impression from reading brahminical tellings of this tale. They refer to his rule as a dark and evil time. But the stories that have persisted in the hearts of subjugated people paint a picture of what life might have been like in Maveli's kingdom. Some say that there were no classes or castes, let alone class rule, nor gender discrimination. Equality, prosperity, peace, crimelessness and good health, are all attributed to this time. There was neither mendacity nor deception, no fake measures or weights in shops. Indeed, absence of every form of malfeasance was the hallmark of Maveli's rule. The special privileges that suras and brahmins claimed for themselves until then were suspended.

After the war, Maveli began performing yajnas to consolidate his strength. In time he performed ninety-nine of them. The gods, huddled together in a forest, were perturbed. If he was to perform the hundredth yajna, Maveli would become the lord of the three worlds for good. So, Aditi, Indra's mother, approached Brahma for help: he advised her to keep a fast of twelve days for Lord Vishnu. Aditi did as she was instructed, and at the end of the twelve days Vishnu appeared and offered her a boon. She demanded that he take birth as her son and help reinstate the rule of the suras. Thus was born Vamana, the fifth reincarnation of Vishnu.

As Maveli progressed with his yajnas, he generously granted all favours to visitors who came asking. To take advantage of this generosity, Vamana, a dwarfish brahmin boy, went to the palace and told Maveli that he too wanted to perform a yajna. To set up a makeshift shed for the purpose, will His Royal Majesty please part with a piece of land so small that he could measure it in three paces, the diminutive brahmin asked. Bali was embarrassed at hearing what sounded like a trivial request unbecoming of his much-publicised status and wealth. Not suspecting foul play, Bali granted the wish. In a fleeting moment, the small boy assumed cosmic size and in his first two gigantic steps measured the earth and heaven. Vamana then turned to the asura monarch with an expectant look in his eye. Bali understood what this meant. Not one to go back on his word, the king bowed his head, stoically accepting defeat, and the brahmin put his foot on the asura king's head pushing him down into the netherworld. With Bali went all other asuras. As Indra occupied the throne once again, the jubilant gods and brahmin sages showered flowers on him and celebration spread through their ranks. Mahabali who once ruled Kerala remains holed up in the underworld and in Malayali memory.

For Keralites, the important part of the story comes now. Heartbroken at the monarch's defeat, the people irreverently spurned the Vishnu avatar and made a fervent plea to their ruler to visit them every year. Maveli accepted the invitation. Another version goes that Maveli wanted to see his subjects frequently and requested Vamana to grant him the right. Vishnu magnanimously assented. Maveli's departure, his defeat, led to eventual victory: he became the ruler of the hearts and minds of his former subjects whose love and reverence continue to this day. The conspiracy of the gods to deny him immortality only ended up immortalising him. Every year, across the ages, Maveli is eagerly awaited as the people of green Kerala roll out the red carpet for the gentle colossus to stroll along the Malayali mindscape. The arrival of Maveli, pious and avuncular, to a euphoric welcome is the promise of an egalitarian social order that could yet come to pass. The story of a heaven having existed in the past energises the people to dream of a future heaven. Plants and trees and even the great sea (later known as the Arabian Sea) are said to join in in welcoming the gentle ruler.

Festivals often function as a repetition or commemoration of an event in the past. A celebration of something that has already happened. Onam is slightly different. Although it is a remembrance of a lost past, it is also symbolic of the desires of the present and the possibilities of the future. For Malayalis, Onam is the festival of what could have been and at the same time what could very well be. In villages, towns and cities, at home and in the diaspora, this harvest festival rouses a collective frenzy. Onam falls in the Malayalam month of Chingam (August–September.). The previous month, Karkitakam, is marked by shortages. Even so, preparations and the excitement of anticipation is very much in the air. After Karkitakam, the granaries are full and people are afforded a holiday. The appearance of the Attham asterism, which is accompanied by the Atthachamayam procession in Trippunithura off Kochi, marks Onam proper as only ten days away. In some other parts of the state, the subdued merriments in the days that follow Attham, reach a crescendo on Tiruvonam (Tiru-Onam; Holy-Onam) tapering off in the following days. The main celebrations are on the asterism of Shravana. The word Onam perhaps comes from Shravanam.

In Kerala, cultural memory is infused with a sense of loss. Over the decades large sections of the population have left the state looking for better opportunities in other parts of the country and the world. This phenomenon has come to characterise Malayali identity. Onam, then, signals a sense of homecoming. In the unhomeliness of being scattered around the world, Onam sometimes becomes a way of making wherever you are into Kerala. A time to go back home to the motherland, if you can afford it. A time for new clothes, gifts, folk dances, games, friendly wrestling bouts and snake boat races. Traditionally, older people in the family are expected to give gifts to the younger folks. The sumptuous feast prepared for lunch, the sadya, is the central event. In 1960, the then Chief Minister, Pattam Thanu Pillai, declared Onam to be Kerala's 'national festival'. The only time in recent years the Malayali did not celebrate Onam was in 2018 when a devastating deluge that lasted several days resulted in incalculable loss of human and animal life, destruction of crops, houses and other forms of social capital. People organised large-scale rescue missions instead. The floods forced a rethink of the development path the state had chosen. A new way of organising society yet again came to the fore.

In the past, Onam wasn't merely restricted to what we know today as Kerala. People in various parts of South India used to celebrate Onam in the ninth century CE. Judging by the elegant simplicity of the Malayalam that we encounter in Onappattu, a popular ballad, the festival does not go back long in history. The food served is generally vegetarian, but in northern Kerala people prepare meat dishes for the sadya. So it is disingenuous to dub it an upper caste festival. Not that vegetarianism is an exclusively upper caste way of life.

All the noise and glitter of Onam is wilfully contradictory to the injustice perpetrated on a benevolent antigod who paid a phenomenally high price for his commitment to truth and his refusal to depart from his word. There was also a time when Onam did not have the egalitarian character that is assigned to it now. In the feudal times which were marked by trenchant brahminism, Onam was the festival of the overlords, and tenants carried vegetables and fruits to the landlords' homes. With the abolition of land tenancy in 1970, and the decline of feudal land relations, such practices tapered off. Even before this, tenants had been mounting struggles for decades, reclaiming their place as equal human beings, rejecting the shackles that bound them.

But the ownership of Onam remained with the privileged castes. At the temples controlled by colonising brahmin uralans, temple funds were used to feed thread-wearing priests for the festival. Records in Trikkakkara show donation of land to the temple for feeding brahmins. Even now, the feudal and brahminical trappings of the festival are quite obvious.

Onam finds mention in Sangam classics like *Mathuraikanchi.* There are references to the festival in Austrian missionary, Paolino da San Barthalomeo's *A Voyage to the East Indies*, an account of his journey through India between 1776 and 1789 CE. A celebration in honour of Mayan, a Dravidian god who became Vishnu in the wake of Aryan arrival, was marked by feasts where meat was not taboo. Jacob Fenicio, a Portuguese missionary who lived in Kerala between 1584 and 1631, mastered Malayalam and familiarised himself with the social customs and rituals of the people here. He too recorded Onam celebrations in honour of Mahabali. According to Fenicio, people believed that Vishnu banished Maveli, appointed him the gatekeeper of heaven and allowed him to visit the people here once a year. He observed that the festival was a celebration of the utopian rule of Maveli. People wore new clothes and cooked delectable food. Fenicio was also a bosom friend of Ayyappa of Sabarimala, as we will see later. Another festival celebrated later in the year, with the lighting of numerous lamps, marked the freeing of Bali by Vasudeva's consort Lakshmi from the underworld prison where he was languishing. In the puranas there is mention of this day, Deepapradanam, when illumination and flowers decorated the netherworld, all to please Mahabali. Deepapradanam coincides with the North Indian festival of Dipavali or Diwali. Whether Diwali is a morphed form of the Maveli festival, who can say?

Onam's popularity in the rest of South India in the old days is also undeniable. In Tamizhakam it used to be a seven-day festive event. Some Tamil classics contain references to Onam festivities. Mahabalipuram in Tamil Nadu is obviously named after the great king of peasants. However, attempts at erasing and brahminising this past are obvious. A Mahabalipuram tourism website claims that Mahabali was a rude and cruel king who was killed by Vishnu, and the place was given its 'actual' name, Mamallapuram, by the Pallavas. Maveli-related celebrations were once popular in the Karnataka and the Deccan regions as well.

The reason for this popularity perhaps lies in the material nature of the festival. It being a harvest festival, Onam and its allied practices must have bled into or accumulated from existing harvest celebrations. Decidedly it emerges from the village. Colourful flowers are as inseparable from the event as the clothes and the food. Time was when boys and girls joyfully went about, exploring the wild, to gather flowers to prepare the traditional flower carpets. Flower decorations find mention in the works of Benjamin Ward, Peter Connor and William Logan. Some think the festival has its roots in the fertility cult which aims at the prosperity of the people—higher food grain production and creation of more wealth.

Digging deeper into all the paraphernalia that now surrounds Onam, its being a part of the subaltern culture is quite clear. Some of the pulaya Onam songs are loud expressions of indignation and retribution. In northern Malabar, Maveli comes as Oneswaran, also known as Onappottan. The tribal malaya community, after ten days of rigorous penance, reserve the right to enact the role of Onappottan in the first two days of the four-day festival. With a painted face, white beard, colourful attire, and a palm leaf umbrella, announcing his arrival with a loud bell, Onappottan goes from house to house, collects rice and paddy and doles out blessings. Aranmula in southern Kerala hosts the snake-boat regatta in the Pampa.

The central Kerala city of Thrissur has its own way of pulling the curtain on the jamboree, suggesting a Muslim connection. On the fourth and final day of Onam, teams of youth coming from surrounding regions, painted up as spotted and striped tigers and leopards, dance their way through the heart of the city. This pantomime–feral dance, which is rightly called pulikkali (tiger dance) is accompanied by howls, growls and drum-beats of wild abandon. Muslims from what is now Tamil Nadu are believed to have brought this popular art form, which was once a feature of Muharram celebrations, into Thrissur. In the dialogue between Jotirao Phule and Dhondiba in the *Selected Writings of Jotirao Phule* there is a reference to Muslims painting themselves as tigers during Muharram. Of late, however, sky-rocketing expenses, shortage of funds and the state tourism department's apathetic attitude towards pulikkali on Chatayam day have reportedly forced many teams to withdraw from participating in the street dance.

Over the centuries, the culture of Bali-worship spread throughout the subcontinent, even as the tyranny of the Vedic tradition grew stronger. There are variants of the myth all about, with slight differences in details and nuances from region to region. In Maharashtra, the popularity of the Bali myth was epitomised in Jotirao Phule's retelling, where 'Bali Raj' was envisaged as a past utopia destroyed by brahminism. Even Jainism, the shramana faith which was a reaction to the divisive casteism, meaningless ritualism and superstition of the Vedic religion, has its Bali. Unlike Buddhism, the other profoundly non-theistic creed that posed a formidable challenge to brahminical Hinduism in the sixth century BCE, Jainism did not reject Hindu myths in toto. The secular trappings—flowers, Oneswaran teyyam, pulikkali, boat race, Onatthallu (Onam wrestling match), besides the profoundly fascinating non-Aryan myth—provide ample material to prove that the Malayali's Onam is a secular subaltern festival.

Mahabali's capital

Trikkakkara, it is believed, was Mahabali's capital where he was to conduct his last yajna to gain control of the three worlds. Although the deity that sits in Trikkakkara's temple is Vamana, here Tiruvonam is Mahabali's day. Besides cultural programmes, the day sees a ritual feast for thousands. The folk tradition having consistently revered Mahabali, it is possible that he was a non-Hindu god before being hijacked into the brahmin myths as happened in the case of many subaltern deities. There is a belief that the brahmin colonialists overthrew a Buddhist ruler, demolished the vihara and built a Hindu place of worship in Trikkakkara. The Aryans saw to it that the non-Hindus' harvest festival, the most important festival of the year, coincided with the celebrations in the new temple.

You will find 'Trikkakkarappans', 'lords of Trikkakkara', made of soiled mud, in the courtyards of homes during Onam. K.T. Ravivarma (2001) says Trikkakkara was originally Tiru-kal-karai, translatable as land of (Vamana's) three holy feet.

It is also possible that the temple here was built by Vaishnavites in the eighth century. History vouches for the fact that the role of this shrine in promoting the Vaishnava cult was enormous. In the days of the second Chera empire (circa fifth century CE), the ruling Kulashekharas used to celebrate Onam in Trikkakkara on a grand scale for twenty-eight days. The Chera emperor and naduvazhis (local chieftains) used to attend these celebrations. For the Chera ruler, Onam was less a festival than an opportunity to keep in touch with local chieftains to guarantee continued loyalty and allegiance to the empire. In 2017, the Travancore Devaswam Board, which looks after the Trikkakkara temple, decided to set up a bronze stature of Mahabali near the shrine. The right-wing Hindu Aikya Vedi protested, but the board chief put his foot down. He, however, went on to Hinduise the mythology: though he was an asura, Maveli was a devotee of Vishnu, he proclaimed. The Hindu Aikya Vedi leader agreed half-heartedly. But there is an unanswered question: had Maveli been a Vishnu devotee, would there have been a Vamana avatar? It takes being especially deceitful to claim that the principled loser became the willing vassal of the unprincipled victor after a war.

The legion of Malayalis working in other Indian cities do not lag behind in celebrating Onam. Those who do not have the time and money to return home, arrange public celebrations and feasts at a convenient place on a convenient day: sometimes on the next holiday if Tiruvonam falls on a working day. This migrant population often proudly claims its celebration to be even more of an enthusiastic welcome to the asura monarch than by those in Kerala. They labour under a double nostalgia, both for the days of Maveli and for their homeland. In Delhi, Malayali organisations arrange their own cultural functions on a grand scale in various parts of the city, including in the Jawaharlal Nehru University campus, a stronghold of the radical left and home to the country's budding intelligentsia. Professors mix with students freely in cooking the traditional Onam feast.

In the eighth–ninth century, at the time of the decline of Buddhism and Jainism accompanied by the rise of assertive Vaishnavism, Vamana was elevated to the status of god. Vaishnava monks would celebrate the festival with prayers and devotional songs. In one of his poems, Perialvar, the Tamil Vaishnavite poet-propagandist, who lived around the same time, writes about Onam as the celebration of Vamana's victory over Mahabali. By floating the Vamana Jayanthi theory, brahminism seeks to rob the subalterns of what remains of their cultural capital.

In Kerala too there have been attempts to install Vamana in the popular imagination, replacing Mahabali, and give the festival a façade of a brahminical foundation. Hindu spokesmen like Vatakkumkoor Rajaraja Varma, author of *Kerala Samskrita Sahitya Charitram*, have maintained that the festival is a celebration of Vamana's birthday. He justified Vamana's action in sending Mahabali to the netherworld as comeuppance for the asura king's 'grabbing' of land belonging to the devas. All this was part of an attempt to escape the embarrassment of welcoming the enemy of their gods. They wanted to shift this 'disobedient' paradigm in the cultural life of Kerala and build up Hindu nationalism. The Malayali, however, has always been scornfully dismissive of the elite theory that Vishnu incarnated as Vamana to save 'dharma'.

The first vague reference to the Bali myth appears in the Rig Veda, the earliest of the four Vedas, produced around 1500 BCE. In the Rig Veda, however, there is neither Vamana nor Bali. As Indra's sidekick, it is Vishnu himself who takes the three giant steps, creating three worlds because the population had multiplied and the people needed fresh pastures and land for habitation. Thus, the objective behind his action seems to be the welfare of the people and prosperity—not elimination of asuras. The proverbial animus between devas and asuras was still far away. The three steps he took earned Vishnu the name 'Trivikrama'. Later, in the Brahmanas (1000–600 BCE) the dwarf boy is introduced, but he is Vishnu in disguise and not an avatar. Here Vamana takes the three steps and defeats the asuras to seize land for the gods, but once again there is no mention of Bali. It is in the Mahabharata that for the first time we come across Vishnu's dwarf avatar doing a 'trivikrama' to usurp the asura emperor's kingdom.

The Incarnations

Let us take a cursory look at Lord Vishnu's incarnations. The Sanskrit word 'avatar' indicates the lower form into which the Supreme Being descends to achieve a particular mission. Every incarnation of Vishnu, as we learn from charioteer Krishna when he tells it to Arjuna in the Kurukshetra battlefield, had the objective of finishing off the wicked, saving the virtuous and establishing dharma. The avatars emerged in the context of the regular battles between the asuras and the devas, which have been portrayed as a confrontation between good and evil but was in fact a struggle between brahminical Hinduism which upheld caste and the people-oriented shramana culture. The avatars were an answer to one of the challenges that Hinduism faced from Buddhism and Jainism. The doctrine of incarnations, which finds mention in the Bhagavad Gita, was an effective way to establish brahmin hegemony and also gave Vaishnavism its peculiar power. In the modern era, wild claims are made about how the ten avatars anticipate the Darwinian theory of evolution.

The avatar stories were partially contributed by pre-Aryan myths. The first four avatars of Vishnu belonged to the Krita Yuga; Vamana, Rama and Parasurama to the Treta Yuga and Krishna and Balarama to the Dwapara Yuga. At the end of the last kalpa (the length of a single cycle of creation and destruction of the universe), Hayagriva stole the Vedas from the hands of

Brahma who had fallen asleep, and hid the tome under the celestial ocean. Vishnu then incarnated as Matsya (fish), slayed the horse-headed asura and retrieved the Vedas. In the second incarnation, during the churning of the ocean by the devas and asuras to obtain the elixir of immortality, the king of tortoises offered his back as a pivot on which to rest Mount Mandara, which acted as a churning stick. The Varaha (boar) avatar killed Hiranyaksha, the asura who stole the Vedas, and recovered the oeuvre and the earth from the bottom of the ocean. Asura patriarch Hiranyakashipu was furious that his son Prahlada was an incorrigible Vishnu acolyte. "Is your lord present here?" asked Hiranyakashipu pointing to a pillar, and the son nodded. The senior asura cut the pillar and out emerged Narasimha—half man, half lion. Hiranyakashipu who had wangled a unique boon from Brahma, that neither man nor beast could kill him, neither during day nor at night, neither inside the house nor outside, neither on earth nor in the air, suffered a gory end, at the hands of one who was neither man nor animal but one with the body of a man and face of lion, who disembowelled the asura with his claws, at dusk, on his lap, on the threshold. The fifth avatar was Vamana and the sixth Parashurama. About both of them in detail later.

The seventh avatar was Rama, slayer of Ravana who abducted his wife, Sita. Rama was followed by the colourful Krishna, who was secreted away as an infant and grew up in his new home into a naughty prankster, a seducer of many a young cowherd, and Arjuna's bosom friend. He survived a number of attempts on his life, subdued the dreaded serpent Kaliya in the Yamuna, and killed his maternal uncle. The ninth avatar is Balarama, Krishna's peacenik elder brother. Kaurava prince Duryodhana's guru in the use of the club, Balarama decided to go on a pilgrimage even before the conch shells sounded in the Kurukshetra battleground. The last and tenth avatar, Kalki, is yet to come—mounted on a white horse, to finish off 'barbarians' and atheists in this 'age of decline'.

After killing Hiranyakashipu, Narasimha anointed the slain asura's god-fearing son Prahlada as king. After Prahlada, his son Virochana took over and after him his son Bali became the king and ruled the land till Vishnu packed him off to the netherworld. Vedic Hinduism later incorporated the Buddha as an avatar of Vishnu. For this Balarama was removed from the list of the dasavataras.

People have interpreted the Vamana myth variously. For one thing, short stature indicates deception. Again, the story possibly has a lot to do with the migration of the Aryans from the West Punjab region to the Gangetic plains. The myth has also been linked to natural phenomena; according to Bal Gangadhar Tilak, one of the leaders of the national movement from Maharashtra who authored a tome defending the Bhagavad Gita, Vishnu's three giant steps symbolise the sun's annual movement. For him, the growing in size of the short-statured Vamana symbolises the mild morning sun, which, as the day advances, not only dispels darkness but also shines in full effulgence and heats up the earth. It is also claimed to denote a tiny embryo that has tremendous potential for growth.

To prove that the Indian attitude to life is more materialist than spiritual, some scholars point to the country's festivals. There is hardly anything spiritual or religious about festivals. There is, in fact, a trade-off between material prosperity and festivals; Diwali, Dussehra, Navaratri, Onam invariably follow a bountiful harvest creating a milieu which brings people closer, creating a suitable atmosphere for social and economic interaction.

Though a people's festival, Onam is also easily commodified in mass culture as kitsch. Folk art grows from below, while mass culture is imposed from above. Much of the earthy significance of the festival makes way for capitalist and consumerist appropriation that inevitably infect our senses and our attitude towards the world. Onam no longer remains the flight to freedom it promised in the past. More often, it becomes an excuse to rake in a handsome profit through whopping liquor sales.

For the trading class, a mighty presence in Kerala, Onam is a literal godsend. The whole idea of Onam celebrations, with gifts of clothes and feasts, must have originated in the mind of the merchant. Malayalis are expected to sell even land to celebrate Onam. In this, the repetition of Mahabali's gesture becomes all too real. In the last few decades the market has intensified its stronghold on a peasants' festival. Gone are the days when children would roam around and collect flowers and display beautiful designs in front of every home and institution. Flowers also are now commodities to be purchased in shops. The market finds in Maveli a useful mascot who, with the help of a business-friendly media, palms off motor cars, two-wheelers, laptops, mobile phones, clothes, jewellery, food items—anything you can dream of, to keep you occupied, distracting you from the task of problematising the multiplicity of power relations we find ourselves caught in. In colourful advertisements the darling of the common people and exemplar of justice appears as a corpulent and paunchy patriarch of the joint family of the past. This is also the time for salary advance to state government employees, 'bumper editions' of weekly magazines overflowing with advertisements, a surfeit of 'attractive rebates' on clothes and other consumer items.

On the eve of Onam, the kitchen in Malayali households

used to be a beehive of activity. To serve the Onassadya (Onam feast) meant early preparations, hours of labour to prepare the food for all to enjoy. With the break-up of the joint family, the old gendered power dynamic in the family was threatened, but the invisible hand of the market swooped into the drawing room and the kitchen via television channels, and Onam has been reduced into a mere orgy of consumption, while also maintaining old relations undisturbed. Agriculture in Kerala being on the deathbed for all practical purposes, the people here wait for vegetables grown in neighbouring Tamil Nadu just as they do for dishes like sambar, aviyal, olan and kalan from hotels and catering agencies, if they can afford it.

Nevertheless, Onam is not every Malayali's bowl of sweet dessert. The Synod of Diamper held at Udayamperur in June 1599, which was an attempt by the Vatican to maintain the religious purity of Kerala Christians, declared Onam to be a Hindu festival and barred the faithful from participating in the festival. For the same reason a fringe group of Islamic fundamentalists sought to bar Muslims from the Onam celebrations. The Maveli myth can be explained from various perspectives. The dalits are divided over celebrating the festival. One section, for example, takes the government and cultural organisations to task for squandering crores to celebrate a festival that tells the story of a great deception, of the assassination of their king by the upper castes. As part of this realisation, organisations like the Indian Dalit Federation have observed hunger strikes during Onam. In Maveli one sees a Dravidian mascot who lost out to the Aryans, and in their radical actions groups such as these stay truer to the spirit of Onam than any of the false festivities of the upper and middle classes.

2

From Primitive Communism to Landlordism

SEVERAL attempts at understanding the evolution of the social life of Mavelinadu have been made. One theory came from E.M.S. Namboodiripad, influenced by the historical materialist understanding of the world: '[Originary tribal] society neither knew any inequality based on castes, communities or classes, nor did it have any relation of superiority and inferiority between man and woman. Such a society is still living in the folklore of Kerala as the 'regime' of Maveli... Such a prehistoric society is known to have existed all over the world and is known in Marxist terminology as 'primitive communism" (Namboodiripad 2010). Understanding society in this manner was an attempt to resuscitate a lost time when humans weren't alienated from the production process, or even from an organic social life. Orthodox Marxism was premised on the belief that an authentically non-alienated society was possible, and even could be said to have existed. A holism that granted to human life an organic character as a simple continuation of nature. Nature itself was assumed to be in a state of harmony and balance.

Such reductionism was later challenged by theories which saw the dynamics of society as more complex, with various forms of oppression separately taking root. For instance, Sharad Patil argued that the Engelsian concept of a primitive communist society was not valid for India where gynocracy (the political supremacy of women) had existed in the past (Patil 2012). The Marxian view allegedly gave short shrift to the subaltern and gender perspective. By situating Vamana within the teleology of materialism, did E.M.S. prevent the formation of an anti-brahmin consciousness in Kerala?

It is important to note that myths, such as those of Maveli, and concepts such as 'primitive communism' serve a similar purpose. In telling a story of the past, they betray, or rather divulge, the basic maxims of how they assume society ought to be arranged. There is therefore a long history of successive Marxist scholars who identify specific instances in history as moments in the egalitarian dream of communism. Some miss the mark to embarrassing extents, like when S.A. Dange endorsed a book which claimed that Vedanta Hinduism was the epitome of communism. Others note that it was the Buddhist period which saw the proliferation of communistic life in India. This, they said, was because there existed an essentially collective decision-making process and therefore the state, if one existed, was far from authoritarian. The means of production were primitive, but democracy and freedom thrived. Such projections into the past often widely missed the mark and led to much grand-standing, with claims like 'there was no gender discrimination … there was no exploitation … all were happy.' Not only are such 'truths' hard to ascertain, one can be fairly certain that they are untrue. Nevertheless, the point Marx was trying to make by historicising class relations was to locate the emergence of surplus production. On one level, it is undeniably true that a surplus of commodities wasn't produced by communities of the distant past who could produce just enough for their immediate needs. Capital's need to reproduce itself by draining every ounce of surplus value from commodities was a tendency that evolved with time, and which was provably exploitative and unnecessary. The point was to change this dynamic by revealing its contingency in history and to demystify its hold on our imagination as necessary. For such an exercise of rethinking the relations of the world, rethinking of the past also becomes necessary. In this sense, myths too reveal and can be weapons in fortifying the consciousness of historically exploited peoples thus giving a clarion call to a world that it is to come.

Looking at mythical examples, then, which provide glimpses at a kind of egalitarian life, may be scorned at, yet they shouldn't be cast aside precisely because of their potential in helping shape a popular consciousness of dissidence and difference.

The 'manrams' or small village communities that flourished in Kerala in the Mauryan era are an example of such a lost egalitarianism. Each 'manram' was home to a single clan bound together under the auspices of a sacred tree. This tree was held as a totem. Cutting it down was unthinkable. Under this tree the villagers toiled, equal by virtue of their shared struggle against nature, a shared instinct for survival. In the manram, there was no scope for whiling away time constructing complex, rigorously exploitative social structures: there was work to be done. They were similar to the self-reliant village communities that Marx references in his historical writings on India. Communal production and communal consumption were predominant. The central form of livelihood was the breeding of animals and not agriculture, despite the availability of metal. An agricultural economy had hardly developed—Kautilya's Arthashastra mentions gold, jewels and pearls among the commodities that came from Kerala, but not agricultural goods.

Manrams were a sort of tribal republic that hadn't yet transitioned into the monarchical state. Important matters including personal disputes used to be discussed periodically in meetings where the entire clan gathered to make decisions collectively. Elders in the families controlled the manram proceedings in which there was active participation of every family. Such tribal clans came to be called gotras which were further united into ganas: whether the name 'gotra' is a result of subsequent influx of caste ideology or whether brahminism appropriated it from existent culture is difficult to ascertain. Nevertheless, the regulatory and rigid gender norms hadn't yet come to be, and roles in the family weren't stable. One only need look at the European history of 'witch-hunting', a medieval practice through which the power of women as doctors and spiritual teachers was stripped away by a burgeoning monarchy to subjugate them and thus stabilise the system. A similar account can also be given about women in pre-brahminical society.

Such life was soon faced with multiple threats. Change in the nature of forces of production is fertile ground for the proliferation of inequality, despotism and of course foreign occupation. Vamana's three steps then symbolise the first act of primitive accumulation in India, an act of appropriation of communally owned property to benefit a handful. It is doubtful that the primitive, egalitarian society we like to imagine would have sustained itself in the absence of an external onslaught. That internal contradictions were already too large within its fold is probably true. Nevertheless, it was an outside force that was instrumental in the collapse of the Maveli paradigm leading to 'social reorganisation', the particular aspects of subjugation that evolved can undeniably be attributed to this invading force, of brahmin domination and sacral caste hierarchy. Once the simpler modes of production yielded place to the large-scale, antagonistic mode, a tiny minority came to own and control the means and instruments of production. The majority ceased to own any means except their labour power, physical and mental, which they were forced to sell to sustain themselves.

Going by the orthodox theory of historical materialism, primitive communism is followed by slavery, feudalism, capitalism, socialism and finally communism. However, Marx theorised that in India primitive communism made way for the Asiatic mode of production: an empty signifier in the Marxist lexicon that stood for all the variant material developments in the world. The Rig Veda and other tomes provided the cultural foundation for the new social order undergirded by chaturvarnya. Later the feudal caste system replaced the varna order.

Kerala was no stranger to slavery either. The East India Company, too, owned slaves in Malabar. In 1819, the number of slaves in northern Kerala, most of them pulayns and cherumans, was estimated to be around one lakh. As recently as in the nineteenth century, there was brutal caste slavery in Travancore. Slaves were exchanged as gratis in dealings of land. They were given away as gifts and dowry, and were even used to pay off debts. Slave trade also resulted in separation of parents from children, wife from husband, families ripped apart without trace or lineage. A memorandum submitted to the maharaja of Travancore by Christian missionaries in 1836 said that slaves constituted ten per cent of the population in the province. Being intertwined with caste, slavery was particularly harsh and barbaric. Those who violated social rules and taboos were also automatically made slaves. Punishments like amputation of organs was common even for minor slips. Owners had the right to kill thier slaves, and a slave's child was a slave from birth.

Very often the package of donations to brahminical temples also included dalit slaves. The poems of Poykayil Appachan, a crusader against the caste system, were birthed in this milieu. Born in 1879, Poykayil Yohannan, later known as Poykayil Appachan, was a dalit firebrand who worked for the uplift of his community and initiated many legislative reforms. His poems are remembered to this day, especially for their rejection of the past and the imagining of many futures.

> No, not a single letter is seen
> On my race
> So many histories are seen
> On so many races
>
> Scrutinize each one of them
> The whole histories of the world
> Not a single letter is seen
> On my race
>
> There was no one on this earth
> To write the history
> Of my race in the olden days
> What a pity!
>
> Think of it
> Regret fills within
> Let me add something
> In my own melody
>
> The story of
> A people who lived in Kerala
> Since the ancient times
> And how they became demons
>
> No shame have I
> To say the faults of my caste

Though all blame me
A cursed offspring on earth

How is it possible
That all blame us
Till the end
Of earth and sky

How can God
Who shaped everything
Allow this to happen
On earth today?

(Translated by Ajay Sekher)

The pulayans and parayans were the backbone of Kerala's wetland paddy cultivation before the ban on slave trade in 1855. The upper caste farmers feared that if the pulayans were to gain modern education, few would be available to slave in the fields. For this reason, Kolathiri, the ruler of North Kerala, pleaded with the king of Portugal in 1507 not to convert tiyya toddy-tappers and marakkan fishermen to Christianity.

Sanal Mohan's analysis of slavery in Kerala throws light on the social system of the colonial years (Mohan 2015). Slavery was historically organised to generate a free labour force mainly in the agrarian economy. In Kerala, this ancient phenomenon is linked to the caste system, unlike the enslavement of the African community by the colonising West, which was a modern phenomenon. The missionaries who mobilised opinion against slavery did not dig deeper into the organic continuity of caste and slavery legitimised by Hinduism, even as they hinted at such a nexus. The mode of production also remained largely unchanged until the colonial masters reorganised agriculture to suit their interests. Therefore, even after slavery was abolished by a royal order in 1855, untouchable slaves in Travancore remained slaves. They could not own any land, even after becoming 'free', because the root cause of the problem was left untouched.

Brahmin Influx

The sixth avatar of Vishnu, Bhargavarama, born to the brahmin sage Jamadagni and his kshatriya spouse Renuka set out to outdo Vamana in trickery and deceit. Bhargavarama, better known by the name Parashurama because parasu (battle axe) was his famed weapon, stood at the southern tip of the country at Kanyakumari and flung his axe along the western coast towards Gokarna in the north. As the sea retreated, Parashurama reclaimed the land covered by the weapon and gifted it all to the brahmins.

There is a tendency to look for a chronological sequence in the story of avatars. How could Maveli rule over Kerala and be overthrown by Vamana, the fifth avatar of Vishnu, if the land was created, as the myth says, from the sea by Parashurama, a later-sixth-avatar? There are other contradictions too. How could Krishna and Balarama be Vishnu's avatars and contemporaries? In the Ramayana, Parashurama confronts Rama when he breaks king Janaka's bow, and both Ramas are Vishnu avatars!

Parashurama was also an ardent devotee of Lord Siva. This avatar mentored such stalwarts of the Mahabharata as Drona, Bhishma and Karna. His much-publicised gift of land to the brahmins was for expiation of his sins. And his sins were frighteningly stark. There was, for example, matricide: suspecting Renuka's chastity, a livid Jamadagni ordered his sons to kill her, but all of them refused, except Parashurama. Jamadagni turned his four disobedient sons into stones. In return for his loyalty, however, a shrewd Parashurama extracted a few boons from his father, one of them being new life for his mother and four brothers. Jamadagni obliged his dutiful son.

The story of Parashurama's land gifts to brahmins is contained in the *Keralolpatti*, a fifteenth century Malayalam text which glorifies namboodiri hegemony under the guise of telling Kerala's history and is of no historical value. The Parashurama myth, however, reveals the material underpinnings of changes in society. The fib gave a divine aura to the land-owning brahmin, whose position in the agrarian economy remained largely unchallenged for centuries. From the fifth century to the ninth there was large-scale Aryan migration to regions that now form Bengal, Assam, Orissa, Gujarat and Maharashtra. There was also an exodus of Sanskrit and Prakrit speakers from North India to the South along the western coast (Joseph 2019). The first batch of Aryans, which included Buddhists and Jains, besides brahmins, came in the third century BCE, by land and sea. The brahmins looked down upon manual labour, so brought groups of shudra workers to slave on the land. The Sangam era work *Akananooru* by Maturai Maruthan Ilanakanar mentions that Cellur, present Thalipparamba in North Kerala, witnessed new sources of income and new gods. The reference obviously was to the arrival of labourers, the plough, and Vedic Hinduism. During the Sangam era, the Parashurama legend strong in their collective memory came to be accepted as history. In a society which was yet to emerge from its tribal status, the Aryans introduced never-before-seen farming techniques. Consequently, with a boost in agriculture, brahmins gradually became a powerful socio-economic force. The Aryan flotsam settled down in sixty-four villages—thirty-two in Kerala, on the fertile plains on the banks of the Pampa, Perar, Periyar and Bharatappuzha, and as many others in the South Canara region. By the eighth century CE, sprawling urban settlements emerged. The Aryan migrants brought not only the plough and new agricultural methods but also the caste system, a ritualistic temple culture and caste-derived patriarchy into Kerala.

The brahmin migration happened by design rather than by accident. In the North, the Mauryans pursued a conscious policy of dissemination of what they believed to be a superior material culture birthed in the Gangetic basin. Kautilya, Chandragupta Maurya's minister and author of Arthashastra, spelt out the details of their migration plan. The Aryans first came to Vidarbha from where sage Agastya, along with the king of Vidarbha, led a humungous contingent of brahmins to what is now Tamil Nadu. Brahmins in Kerala swear by Parashurama, while Agastya is a popular icon of their Tamil counterparts. At a session of the faculty and students of the school of social sciences of Gujarat University on 17 December 1960, Sangh parivar ideologue M.S. Golwalkar made the outlandish statement (Islam 2015) that North Indians were sent to Kerala to improve the breed of the local Hindus!

The period from the ninth century CE to the early decades of the twelfth, the era of the Chera kingdom of Perumals with their capital at Mahodayapuram, saw the stabilisation of brahmin power and hegemony. In the absence of a sound administrative set-up and strong reserve army, Chera suzerainty over local rulers was limited and they were subject to the whims of the Pandyas and the Cholas. On various issues the Perumals dutifully went by the advice of the brahmins, even to the extent of atoning for having offended them.

The kings and local rulers were expected not to tax the brahmins. Nor could a brahmin be punished if he was found guilty of a serious crime. Even in the later Sangam era protection of the brahmin was considered the responsibility of the rulers.

Death sentence used to be passed on those who killed a brahmin or a cow. The rulers of Edappilly and Chempakassery were themselves brahmins. Following the decline of the Chera kingdom in 1124 CE, the settlements began to amass more and more wealth and exert greater influence in social and political life. The collapse of the Chera kingdom meant freedom to umpteen small chieftains.

Temples, Land

During the first half of the Sangam era, the golden era of Tamizhakam, caste hadn't taken the brutal hold it would go on to take. Every individual regardless of the varna or gender had the right to seek and obtain education, for instance. Women could engage in the work of their choice. The Chera rulers welcomed members of the bardic panan community into their courts. Gifted poets like Kapilar, Pananar and Ouvayar who belonged to this community were regarded as superior to the brahmins and enjoyed high positions in royal courts. The rulers and chieftains used to honour people engaged in various kinds of handicrafts and those toiling in the fields with expensive gifts. The new Aryan rulers who swore by chaturvarnya gave the quietus to the universal education of the pre-Aryan days. Various sections of the population were enlisted in the service of the settlements both as tenants and servants. It was non-brahmins' land that was donated to brahmins in the period from the ninth century to the twelfth. A part of the tax and fine collected from non-brahmins and non-Hindus was squandered on festivals and, again, gifted to brahmins. Since the brahmins were not taxed, for revenue the state had to rely on tax from the common people. Naturally there was a steady decline in the economic status of the toiling masses.

Till the influx of the brahmins from the North, the people here had no formal religion. The worship of godheads, ancestors, heroes and anti-heroes fulfilled their spiritual needs. The brahmins mystified spirituality. During the period from the ninth century to the eighteenth, temples were a powerful economic and political force. As the nerve centre of the economy, they were a savage exploiter of those who worked on land. The common people were kept alienated from the temples. They watched wide-eyed as the migrants performed havans and yajnas, with chants of mantras and animal sacrifices. Sanskrit remained the language of liturgy among the Aryans. The scholars and men of letters among the migrants persuaded the non-brahmins to conduct yajnas or sacrifices for the sake of their own long life and prosperity. The influential work of the scholar Frits Staal, in the 1960s and 1970s, which include several books (and one documentary film) on the Vedas, their chanting, and the fire ritual, derive from time spent with the namboodiris. Kerala's brahmins were considered to be the finest bearers of the Vedic Aryan tradition (Staal 1961).

The subsequent period saw the flowering of a temple-centred brahmin culture. Buddhist viharas and pre-Aryan kavus got converted into temples. Many mega shrines like those in Sucheendram, Thiruvananthapuram, Thiruvanchiyur, Ettumanur and Thrissivaperur (Thrissur) were built in the eighth century. Land owners and the common people funded the construction of the shrines, but their management was in the hands of committees consisting mostly of brahmin uralar (landlords). Brahmins alone could consecrate deities and perform puja. This remained the rule for the next many centuries. The temples acquired huge gold treasures. The Tiruvalla temple in South Kerala, for example, owned a vast quantity of gold, not to mention large tracts of land. The temple in Peruvanam south of Thrissur owned a lion's share of the countryside and the forests.

Hefty donations poured in even from distant Ceylon, for use in temples, including for the feeding of namboodiris. The temple became the centre of many social activities. Sculpture, wall painting and other forms of art were encouraged. Even public utility services like hospitals and banking were provided by the temple. Often, the right to extract taxes was also made over to them. The historian Kesavan Veluthat argues that 'The temple developed as the hub around which activities of production and distribution revolved; it was the temple that decided the pattern in which the institution of caste evolved and got congealed....The temple even developed into a centre of political activity, both as a semi-autonomous entity within the territory of a local chieftain and also as the points behind which the different locality chiefs rallied. In short, the temple, which was the nucleus of the Brahmana settlement, functioned as the agency which transformed the way of life in Kerala--in terms of economy, society and polity' (Veluthat 2013). The period from the ninth century to the eighteenth was the golden age of temples, as they grew in prominence dwarfing even the state in its political importance. Only in the eighteenth century did Martanda Varma, the king of Travancore, and Sakthan Thampuran, the ruler of Cochin, attempt to rein in the temples.

Control over the temples enabled the brahmins to acquire vast tracts of land. A committee, doubling as the village assembly, brokered property allotment both for the temple and the community at large. In the beginning, the committees included both brahmins and non-brahmins, elected for a term of one year. In such a situation the emergence of corruption and opportunism was but expected. Some individual uralar families were able to tighten their control of both the devaswam (temple) and brahmaswam (family) properties. Their term got extended regularly ultimately turning these institutions into private property that the uralars kept for themselves. With this whatever little pretence of democracy this body could boast of also fell. For nearly two centuries preceding the regime of Marthanda Varma, the Sree Padmanabha Swamy temple in Thiruvananthapuram was managed by an outfit called Ettarayogam—'ettara' meaning eight and a half, eight brahmins and one nair.

Chanakya's Arthashastra declared brahmins as bhudevas—gods on earth. Entitlement to land gifts, known as brahmadeya, and control over religion became commonplace for brahmins and these privileges had the putative sanction of the scriptures. In Kerala, land came under the brahmins' possession in various ways. The myth about Parashurama's land gifts symbolised the donation of huge estates of land and villages by the Chalukyas, Pallavas and Kadambas to brahmins. Believing that a brahmin's blessing brought divine grace, the rulers brought over brahmin families from distant lands and donated sprawling estates to them for performing yajnas. Parayars, both men and women, were property to be given away as gifts along with the land.

There is a general agreement among historians that brahmins employed various unfair means to acquire land. A. Sreedhara Menon (2012) alleges that the brahmin trustees mismanaged temple properties and endowments and enjoyed all the revenues therefrom: '[D]uring a critical phase of the Chola-Chera war of the 11th century several ordinary tenants who owned lands and properties transferred their possessions in toto to the Namboodiri Brahmins and the temples because lands and endowments thus made over came to be looked upon as brahmaswams and devaswams and enjoyed freedom from devastation by enemy forces as well as exemption from the payment of tax to the state'. By early twelfth century, the idea that all land belonged to the brahmins, who formed hardly one per cent of the population, was accepted as a home truth. Various sections of the population were enlisted in the service of the settlements both as tenants and servants. A part of the tax and fine collected from non-brahmins and non-Hindus was squandered on festivals and, again, pocketed by the brahmins.

The near total ownership of land and control over religious life, with knowledge of Sanskrit and Sanskrit mantras, enabled the brahmins to extend their grip over all spheres of social and economic life. The Parashurama legend was used to construct an ideological system that would rationalise and perpetuate namboodiri land ownership and hegemony. The settlements managed to reorient a semi-tribal, semi-nomadic society into a temple-centred, agrarian, caste society. Thus was born landlordism. Writes Veluthat: 'The emergence of brahmana landlordism was the culmination of a series of developments in the process of historical evolution. The position of the brahmanas as landlords with command over large tracts of land and tenants and other servants in large numbers entitled them to all feudal privileges. These privileges, together with their sacerdotal offices, placed them at the apex of society. It was this supremacy which influenced the pattern of social and cultural development in Kerala in the years to come' (Veluthat 2013).

It was not entirely by non-violent means that brahmin power expanded in South India. There is a reference in *Keralolpatti* to Parashurama presenting weapons to thirty-six-thousand brahmins to protect Kerala. These brahmins from ten villages came to be known as 'ardhabrahmanas' and 'shastrabrahmanas'. They were exempted from the study the Vedas. In 999 CE the

Cholas attacked Kerala and the conflict between them and the Cheras continued into the eleventh century. The Kulashekharas mobilised all resources for the war. Kantalur salai played a key military role in the conflict in which, *Keralolpatti* claims, thirty-thosand brahmins took part. Military training imparted through temple-supported institutions during the early medieval period apparently resulted in a radical transformation of the social fabric. Their grip on the socio-economic and religious life of the people was soon complete.

Caste segregation

The four-varna structure with the brahmins at the apex was rooted in the transition from a pastoral to a plough-based agricultural economy. According to D.D. Kosambi, an alliance of the Indus priests and their Aryan counterparts worked behind the birth of the endogamous chaturvarnya system. Later the more insidious caste system emerged. Communists saw caste as part of the superstructure which was expected to disappear along with the classes. This has proved a serious misreading of the situation. The inextricable link between caste and land ownership cannot be ignored. Scholar Pradeepan Pampirikkunnu thinks landlordism was built on caste-based production relations and not the other way round. The chronicler of the dalit movement Sunny M. Kapikkad argues that since the nexus between caste and land ownership was ignored, land reforms in Kerala became, in effect, anti-dalit.

Brahmin hegemony in India was buttressed by British colonialism. In the days of the East India Company, Governor-General Warren Hastings gave respectability to local religious traditions as interpreted by obscurantist pandits and maulvis. The British held up caste as the lynchpin of Indian society. The colonial masters thought the brahmins with their knowledge of the scriptures were their best possible intermediaries in this country and internalised the stereotype of the other sections of the colonised being at the bottom in the caste hierarchy.

One of the characteristics of the caste system is the watertight division of labour in the matter of knowledge. It was the exclusive possession of knowledge that enabled the brahmin to grab power and maintain his hegemony for centuries. In a brahmin-dominated society the namboodiris enjoyed a monopoly in religious matters and the right to acquire knowledge. The lower castes' attempts to acquire knowledge were treated as crime. Even the kshatriyas were allowed to gain only a rudimentary education; they were prevented from spreading or developing it. The division of labour was enforced legally by the state. A literate shudra was to be avoided like a drunken man or a mad bull. Apparently to give it legitimacy, *Keralolpatti* claimed that the complex system of caste hierarchy enjoyed the sanction of Adi Sankara.

The namboodiris grew rapidly into a community of revered priests. Variers, marars and poduvals are among the social groups attached to temples, although not as priests. Nairs, though free of distance taboos, were to serve the namboodiris, but were not allowed physical contact. Ezhavas were to maintain a distance of sixteen feet from nairs and namboodiris, pulayas thirty-two feet from ezhavas and nayadis thirty-two feet from pulayas. This distance rule got the stamp of approval at the great Mamamkam, an extravagent religious fair, much like the North Indian Kumbh Mela, which used to be held at Tirunavai once in twelve years.

The untouchables were not allowed to use the roads near the shrines. This proscription continued into the twentieth century, hence the historic satyagraha near the Siva temple in Vaikkam during the time. The government put up 'no-entry for lower castes' notices on roads in the proximity of temples and residences of brahmins. During festivals like the Thrissur pooram, ezhavas and other untouchables who had dwellings on the roadside were required to vacate their houses in order to avoid polluting the procession of brahmins and other upper-caste folks carrying the deity. Even well-to-do, well-educated and prominent ezhavas like C. Krishnan, P. Palpu, P. Velayudhan and Kumaran Asan could not travel on a large number of roads in their provinces.

The popular Onappattu says that after Maveli's downfall, the Aryans found themselves on a higher pedestal than others, what with free food being provided to the twice-born by temples. Under Martanda Varma, an imaginative administrator who brought the Dutch to their knees twice, free dining halls for brahmins mushroomed all over the territory. In Kozhikode, the Zamorin donated paddy fields to the temples so that they could provide free food to the upper castes. Dining halls for brahmins were arranged on special occasions. While this policy spawned a class of parasitical freeloaders, sections of the common people went without food.

Brahmins used to be brought from various parts of South India for the ritual 'murajapam' in the Padmanabha Swamy temple in the heart of Thiruvananthapuram. Murajapam involved the recitation of the three Vedas—Rig Veda, Yajur Veda and Atharva Veda for three hours a day, to finish one round in eight days. Starting in 1744, the murajapam was conducted every six years. In 1750 alone the expenditure on this ritual was estimated to be a staggering two lakh rupees. During the fifty-six-day murajapam, the brahmins were provided with comfortable accommodation and food. Ayurvedic physicians were present to provide medical attention, when necessary. On the face of it, the whole show was conducted to ensure the prosperity of the people and as a form of penance. The areas surrounding the massive temple remained out of bounds for the untouchables. An ezhava lawyer practicing in a court was once caught and sent away to a far-off place. V.T. Raman Bhattathiripad, the brahmin revolutionary who led a crusade against the evils in the community, made a fervent appeal to his namboodiri brethren to boycott the ritual, the expenses for which were being paid by the common man. When the firebrand editor, K. Ramakrishna Pillai, thundered in the newspaper *Swadeshabhimani* that the ruler was expected to see the brahmin and the parayan with the same eye, he was banished from the province. The weekly *Mithavadi* demanded that the lakhs squandered on the ritual be spent to feed the poor.

Marthanda Varma and his six successors, ending with Sreemoolam Tirumal, doled out huge funds to brahmins. In a ritual called hiranyagarbha danam on the occasion of the coronation, the king would get a cow made of gold, enter it through its mouth and come out of the animal's anus, to the accompaniment of mantra chants by brahmins. Later the animal made of gold would be cut into pieces and gifted to the brahmins. Also, in nair families there was a practice of men and women on the deathbed making a ritual gift of a decorated cow, or its price in cash, to a brahmin as a shortcut to heaven.

The namboodiri illams (traditional homes) were bastions of savage patriarchy. It was the starkly patriarchal Manusmriti, written sometime between 200 BCE and 200 CE, that governed the life of the brahmins when they streamed into Kerala. Between the fourteenth and fifteenth centuries the namboodiris shaped a new code known as Lakhudharma Prakashika or

Saankarasmriti which was more regressive and patriarchal than even the Manusmriti. Since Sankara lived centuries before this Sanskrit work was penned, there is no reason to attribute this opus, as some people do, to the acharya of advaita. The author *of* Saankarasmriti was, presumably, some obscure Sankaran Namboodiri who was a Parashurama devotee. It is possible that some brahmins jointly authored Saankarasmriti and attributed it to Adi Sankara to give it divine respectability. For all practical purposes, it governed the day-to-day life of namboodiris till the first decades of twentieth century.

Under the deadweight of the starkly patriarchal Saankara-smriti, women of all castes were barred from gaining or developing knowledge. Brahmin women turned out to be especially tormented victims of the social order fashioned by the brahmins. Married brahmin women are even today called antarjanams—indoors people. Under Saankarasmriti, antarjanams remained just that all through their lives. The new code was mainly a collection of dos and don'ts—more don'ts than dos—which were a manifestation of the impotent power the male brahmin exercised over women in the community. The women were not allowed to appear before strangers and even her grown up in-laws; she could not aspire for education outside home; she could not meet strangers, she could not listen to Vedic chants; she could not walk the streets at night; she could not go to temples while a festival was on; she could not have her nose pierced; so on and so forth. There prevailed a rigid purdah system—while going out the women had to hide themselves under palm leaf umbrellas.

The male brahmin kept a tight leash on female sexuality. Manusmriti treated women in the community as mere sex objects. So did Saankarasmriti. Married women were tasked with breeding and bringing up children. The *Manusmriti* gave brahmin girls the right to choose husbands if their parents could not; Saankarasmriti did not grant even that freedom to the girls. Saankarasmriti prescribed monogamy—the namboodiri was allowed a second marriage only if his wife failed to conceive, but this rule was not followed in practice. As a result, the eldest brother in a family used to be a much-married man. Saankarasmriti rendered the life of the antarjanams drab and colourless; they would spend their cloistered lives in the sombre interiors of gargantuan illams, shackled by mindless rituals and with the name of god on their lips, praying for a long life for her husband. When the husband passed away, which used to happen quite often since many young girls were forced to marry wizened men, life froze for the widow—they would spend the rest of their time rolling prayer beads. Widow remarriage was unheard of. The namboodiri jealously guarded the chastity of his antarjanams. At the slightest rumour about her 'going astray', the woman would be tried in a kangaroo court of family elders, which usually delivered a swift excommunication. In the riveting Malayalam novel *Ummachu* by Uroob (P.C. Kuttikrishnan), we come across an elderly namboodiri who has four wives—two from his own community to beget children, a varier woman for carnal pleasure and a fourth from the royal palace for the status that the kshatriya connection would bestow on him. Besides, he has throwaway relationships with a raft of women from the upper-caste-but-untouchable nair community. A rumour is in the air about an affair between one of his antarjanams and an outsider. In a fit of rage, the namboodiri kills the allegedly guilty wife and he faces death at the hands of her vengeful lover.

The younger brothers in a family were not permitted to marry girls in the same community; they would look for wives in other savarna castes like nairs and variers, in a bizarre liaison arrangement known as 'sambandham' (meaning liaison). Bizarre because his non-brahmin wife or children could not touch him without polluting him, let alone claim a share in his property. That was the aim—averting division of family property. (A rule quoted in the Smriticandrika from the Adi Purana lays down that if a brahmin takes his meal in the company of his low-caste wife, he would lose his caste.) Girls born in kshatriya families too used to be married off to namboodiris. The seed of the brahmin alone will produce good kings, *Keralolpatti* claimed, and so the royal families were not bothered about share in brahmaswam property. It is a sign of the status the brahmin enjoyed in society that despite such humiliating norms nair families prided in having a child fathered by a brahmin. Brahminism is much more than the tyranny of the brahmin. B.R. Ambedkar argued that imposing the caste system on the non-brahmin population was beyond the mettle of the brahmins, even though they were guilty of very, many terrible things. Nor has the malaise of casteism remained confined to Hinduism—it has seeped into Semitic faiths: there are untouchables and brahmins even among the Christians and the Muslims. What is being described as brahminism is not linked solely to the brahmins. 'Brahminism is the very negation of the spirit of Liberty, Equality and Fraternity,' wrote Ambedkar in his seminal work *Annihilation of Caste*. 'Brahminism is practised not just by the brahmin against the kshatriya or the vaishya against the shudra, or the shudra against the untouchable, but also by the untouchable against the unapproachable, the unapprochable against the unseeable. It means there is a quotient of brahminism in everybody regardless of which caste they belong to.'

3

The Great Sacrificer

THE PERSISTENT efforts by brahminic Hinduism to dislodge Mahabali from his iconic perch in social memory have been consistent in their failure. The many-splendoured king continues to stride the Malayali psyche proudly. For the common people of Kerala, Onam is the time to extend a euphoric welcome to the gentle colossus who stands head and shoulders—and not just physically—above his cunning, puny adversary. Bali was the son of Virochana and grandson of Prahlada whose father Hiranyakashipu was slain by Narasimha, the fourth avatar of Vishnu. With the brahmin guru of the asuras, Shukracharya, as his adviser, Bali turned the country into a prosperous land where people lived happy lives. Though a pious Vishnu acolyte, Prahlada is all praise for Mahabali's integrity and honesty. When Maveli bowed before Vamana, he was bowing before his own word that he would fulfill every alms-seeker's wish. He heeded to an inner necessity, which he apparently considered divine, rather than to the voices of Shukracharya and Prahlada, both of whom saw through the gods' devious game and warned that the humble-looking supplicant was no impecunious brahmin boy, that the king would be an unfortunate victim of a conspiracy. Shukracharya tried to foil the donation ritual, but Maveli's virtue proved his undoing. By keeping his word to Vamana, he lost a kingdom but won its people's lasting respect and affection. Not being obscenely obsessed with maintaining a dynamic of power simply because it would be favourable to his person, unlike his unprincipled adversary, the noble ruler refused to resort to unethical means to achieve success. After his successful mission, Vamana broke into a eulogy of the asura king's nobility and generosity.

Heroic warrior and philosopher-statesman, Mahabali was a devotee of Siva, who was originally a pre-Aryan Dravidian god. The shramana ruler was expressly anti-caste and champion of the poor. The Mahabharata provides ample evidence that he was consistently opposed to the chaturvarnya system of social segregation. Indeed, one of the reasons for the gods' animosity to the asura king was his refusal to impose caste distinctions in his land. He had no patience with the stereotypes and shibboleths of brahminism. By his example he demolished brahminism's pet theory that the shramanas were intellectually inferior, that they were unfit to rule and fit only to be ruled. This is the land that people dream of and feel nostalgic for centuries since. As a ruler, he was committed to the asura values which were democratic and people-friendly. That explains the equality that his kingdom could boast of. Mavelinadu was closest to what Jesus Christ wanted to usher in but his followers did not—the Kingdom of Holy Spirit, a land of justice, freedom, fellowship and brotherhood. Phule, the anticaste thinker from Maharashtra, makes a similar comparison between Christ and Mahabali as great men who sacrificed their lives for the greater good. When the government of Kerala decided to set up a string of consumer stores for the people, they were christened, appropriately, Maveli Stores.

Maveli was, mythically if not historically, the first in the long line of mighty icons and mightier iconoclasts—non-brahmin gods, antigods, warriors, social revolutionaries and subaltern intellectuals—who came to be revered. Like them, Maveli represented an alternative culture which is non-conformist and heretical. Jotirao Phule also wrote of how Maveli was a connoisseur of music, and is said to have created the famous Malhar raga.

Mahabali led the asuras during the churning of the primeval ocean. When the devas and the asuras succeeded in extracting the elixir of immortality thanks to their joint efforts, Vishnu bolted with the nectar. What followed was a bloody war in which Bali was badly wounded. The monarch was taken to the palace where sage Agastya revived him. A man of amazing versatility and erudition, who earned praise even from Brahma and Indra, the asura king, despite physical injuries, harangued his arch rival on the relationship between karma and its fruits. Again, realising the gravity of the conspiracy against him after he lost his crown, Maveli confronted Vamana and thundered in righteous rage: 'You have acted against truth and justice. But you can only defeat men, not ideas. The ideas which I popularised here will never fade.' Maveli put to work the Platonic notion, put forward in the classic text, *Republic*, that unless philosophers ruled as kings, or kings and princes were genuine philosophers, there will be no respite from bad days for mankind.

The Onappattu suggests that the lower castes did not accept their place without question and that they did dream of equality and fraternity. The song mentions that the Maveli regime was a byword for socio-economic equality. There was no falsehood, no cheating. There was all-round prosperity. People enjoyed full health, child mortality was unheard of. There was neither waste of food in pujas nor slaughter of animals in yajnas. Maveli's successor arranged free dining halls for brahmins and as a result the common people went without food. Some lines about the brahmins in the Onappattu were allegedly censored out, and it is said that a sanitised version is now circulated. The poem concludes with a fervent prayer for an end to the exploitative value system that Vamana represented and for return of the Maveli regime.

What the monarch's ashwamedha yajna tent witnessed was a clash of values. After the putsch, the Maveli model lay in shreds. The popular Onappattu says that after Maveli's fall, pampering of brahmins began in earnest. The regime in which everyone was equal and no one had any special rights yielded place to a land where misery was the lot of the ordinary people. Indeed, the Vamana-led insurrection led to a decline of all that was noble. Incidentally, other avatars of Vishnu too have cared two hoots about ethical conduct. Rama killed Sambuka, a shudra, for performing Vedic austerities and killed Sugriva's brother Baali who had done him no harm. In the Kurukshetra battlefield Krishna advised Arjuna to kill Karna, when the latter, unarmed, was fixing the wheel of his war-chariot. Violating the rules of war, Bheema struck Duryodhana on the thigh, again on a signal from Krishna. The repeated appearances of Vishnu merely seem to be in order to help spur the immoral actions of immoral people along.

Incapable of malevolence and a bit eccentric perhaps, as a ruler Mahabali was strong, almost invincible, and wielded tremendous power. The name 'Bali' was apparently derived from the word balam, meaning strength. The anti-asura forces were well aware that confronting an outstanding asura monarch of such a high stature would be difficult. Hence no risk was taken. Ending the reign of Mahabali was the sole objective of the Vamana avatar. It was after a thousand-year pregnancy that Vamana was born to Aditi, the mother of the devas; the brahmin boy had to spend long hours in meditation before going to Mahabali; in what should have been a matter of humiliation for a sura, he had to play supplicant before the asura king. Worse, he had to resort to subterfuge and was even apologetic about it. In the netherworld Vishnu ensured that Bali enjoyed a life of all worldly comforts. Vishnu, they say, volunteered to serve under him.

Bali's glory does not fade even in the subsequent births. In the Mahabharata, in reply to a question from Yudhishtira, patriarch Bhishma narrates a story of what happened in a later birth to Bali. Aeons after Mahabali is overthrown and the asura kingdom smashed, Indra goes on a mission to find the perpetual enemy of the devas. Brahma guides him to a poor man's hut where Indra finds a donkey—it was Bali reborn as an animal. Indra did not hide his happiness on seeing the plight of the person who once ruled over the three worlds. He passes snide comments, but Mahabali refuses to be provoked. Brahma chides Indra that it is not proper for the king of devas to mock at Bali. Age, warned Brahma, will take its toll on everyone and would not spare even Indra. The king of gods realises his mistake and, when he leaves, is all praise for the draught animal which was once a great philosopher king.

A popular myth among adivasis in Wayanad is about the primordial soil Maveli kept in custody, its theft by the tampurans (meaning lords), the formation of the earth and finally his annual visit to see the earth and its inhabitants. The tampurans came to visit Maveli. When the king offered them seats and went for his customary bath and dinner, the gods stealthily searched the place and found the soil. They stole the soil and kept small specks of it in coconut shells. When the soil became too big for the coconut shells to hold, it was transferred into baskets. When the baskets were found too small, they were transferred to the store rooms. The process went on and on until, ultimately, they became the Earth. The kurichiars of Wayanad have a tradition of celebrating Onam with a popular folk song. In it, Maveli goes by the name Mavothy. God puts his foot on Mavothy's head and pushes him down to the sea.

The earthen trikkakkarappans, which have a square base and taper off upwards, adorn courtyards of homes in Kerala during Onam; they seem to symbolise the blooming seed. Onam being a harvest festival, trikkakkarappans are a way of thanking the soil. The trikkakkarappan is the idol of the farmer, whose worship is the worship of soil, toil and mother nature. Valiyon of Tamizhakam of the Sangam age was a god of agriculture and a progenitor of Maveli. Baliraja of Maharashtra who is an icon of the marginalised sections carries the plough with him.

In Kasargod and other parts of northern Kerala too, Maveli is a farm deity, representing the spiritual harmony between man and the soil. The welcome to Maveli is accorded here on Deepavali day, two months after the festival of Onam concludes in other parts of the state; he is also known as Polichandran. The myth current here does not say that Maveli was packed off to the netherworld. Some scholars see a 'historical inevitability' in the Mahabali–Vamana face-off. Maveli represented the weakening agricultural economy and the growth of Vamana into a giant represented the rapid expansion of a commercial class with its own value system. It can be interpreted as the victory of a dynamic science and technology over a static religion.

The confrontation is also seen as one between an expanding coloniser state and a people who were, for all practical purposes, self-governing. An indigenous populace was absorbed into a tyrannical system.

On the literary firmament

No mythical figure and no festival have provided so much inspiration to artists, poets and writers in Malayalam as Maveli and Onam. The number of poets, from the ancient to the post-modern, who have written nostalgically about the asura king's benign rule is legion. Tributes are paid in a variety of ways, with writers and scholars subjecting the story to vigorous critical analysis. Nostalgia, happiness, empathy, sympathy, cynicism—there is space for practically every human sentiment and social situation in the literary world surrounding Maveli and his annual visit to Kerala.

There is hardly a Malayalam poet who has ignored Maveli and Onam. P. Kunjiraman Nair, K. Satchidanandan and Vyloppilly Sreedhara Menon are among the modern Malayalam poets who see in Maveli's rule a living metaphor for justice and equality. No poet has been more prolific on Maveli and Onam than Kunjiraman Nair; so much so that he has earned the sobriquet of Mahabali's court poet. The poet is poignantly nostalgic about Maveli's times. He is ever groping for the way to Trikkakkara, the asura king's fabled capital, which, in his eyes, stood for Mavelinadu, the ideal land where there was freedom and love, no one was below or above anyone else, there was neither exploitation nor dishonesty. For Kunjiraman Nair, Onam is a cultural symbol of Malayali sub-nationalism.

The popular comment about Koran, the proverbial dalit labourer (not to be confused with the Islamic religious book), having to content himself with a spoonful of rice gruel during Onam or on the birth of a male child when others were gorging on rich food ("Onam vannalum Unni pirannalum Koranu kumbilil kanji"—Whether it is Onam or the birth of a son/ it's only gruel in the house of Koran) was factually right. In *Onassadya,* Vallathol Narayana Menon laments that the have-nots have always remained deprived of their Onam. *Mabeli Thampuran*, a poem that has come from the pen of Kadathanattu Madhavi Amma, dwells on the asura monarch's visit to an impoverished woman's hovel. However, through folklore the dalits have been recreating their own world during Onam. The credit for most of the Onam songs should go to the subaltern communities.

Akkitham (Achuthan Namboodiri) thinks Onam represents the people's optimism for a better future. In the poignant poem *Mathevarude Kidappara,* Olappamanna shares the concern and sadness of many a poet at the commodification of Onam. The most obvious symptom of this is the Mathevar (the sacred idol of the festival), made of wood and bought from the shop, and kept for future Onams. Earlier the Mathevars used to be made with wet earth every year. With the wooden Mathevar being available in shops, the relationship with the soil is lost for good. In *Idinjupolinja Lokam* (The world that crashed), Olappamanna takes off from Onam to lament the collapse of the welfare state. In Vyloppilly Sreedhara Menon's poem *Thozhilali* the forefathers of the working class are Adam and Eve who were banished from Heaven for defying God's command. In an act of sweet revenge the progeny of the first apostates built, with the sweat of their brow, another heaven on earth. Onam is Malayalis' sweet sentiment and Maveli their honoured guest, says Vyloppilly.

Satchidanandan is right when he says 'the most important movements of subversion—sometimes inversion—in our literature have invoked this prince, this subaltern Mahabali'. As the poet says, Maveli is 'to the people of Kerala the greatest of their princes—a monarch, in some sense an anti-monarch, because he, as a demon king, had been pushed down to the netherworld by Vamana, a Brahmin incarnation of Vishnu, as the gods had become jealous of his just rule and the people's love and respect he enjoyed,' (Satchidanandan 2011). Bali is also a kind of archetypal protagonist of the subaltern dream of an egalitarian society—all the songs about him speak about a time when justice and equality prevailed in the whole community. Perhaps it is our dream of a future projected into the past, a utopia turned into a memory. This Mahabali has been returning to Kerala's culture, art and literature again and again in different periods of our cultural experience.

In a play by Jnanpith laureate G. Sankara Kurup, the old asura king appears as the saviour of the subalterns. 'I am the idea of an idealised world,' Mahabali proclaims. 'A world where there are no *adiyan*s [subjugated] and no *tirumeni*s [high priests]. I remain imprisoned not in the netherworld but in the heart of the world. Please release me; I promise a new world. A world where religion will not stab God in the heart; where art will not hijack life to dark barbarism. There will be light everywhere; Onam everywhere'. In Onakkali, a form of entertainment in southern Kerala, the oppressed sing the lyrics of the nineteenth century dalit leader Pandit Karuppan's *Jatikkummi,* a polemic against the caste system. More significantly, in Anand Neelakantan's fictional work *Asura*, Vamana's mission was expansion of the brahminical knowledge system. He asked for three feet of land in Muziris, the asura capital, to set up a brahminical learning centre. The request was granted and the small centre grew first into a massive missionary institution and then to a hotbed of conspiracy and court intrigue. (Neelakantan 2012) The hierarchical brahminical religion swept away the asura empire.

Not everyone sees the Bali myth in the same way, but the common theme is land grab by deception. Ezhava leader P. Palpu, who was the driving force behind the Kerala Renaissance, introduced elephantiasis and black magic into the myth (Kumar 2004). His interesting theory is that the brahmins who hated Mahabali sent a dwarf from the community who obviously knew a special trick of inducing temporary elephantiasis on himself. He was, therefore, assumed to represent a god. The dwarf went to this ruler and begged for three feet of land for the brahmins. Mahabali gladly granted the demand. The small brahmin went on to perform his secret trick and with his tremendously big feet, measured the whole of the kingdom and a great deal more. 'As he had nothing more to give, the ruler offered his head to keep his word and the brahmin placed his tremendously big elephantoid foot on his head and sent him away as an exile to Batavia or some other island which was then considered to be the antipode.'

As Udaya Kumar points out, in Palpu's version Vamana's transformation into a gigantic, cosmos-filling divine behemoth figure is stripped of its mythological aura and revealed to be a comprehendible trick. 'The illusion produced by magic is identified with the seemingly scientific description of a disease common in many parts of the Kerala coast. However, in order for this translation to work, the size of the elephantoid foot has to be exaggerated beyond all limits of scientific possibility or plausibility.' If the myth relies on implausible exaggeration, so does the alternative account. In India the past used to be recorded in the form of events blown out of proportion. The earliest realistic view of history is in Buddhist and Jain works.

In Anand's short story *Bimbangal,* on Onam day Maveli takes a day off and goes around the universe with his grandfather Prahlada telling him about those like Ravana, who had to face defeat at the hands of the savarnas. Prahlada, a Vishnu devotee who succeeded his father Hiranyakashipu after Narasimha killed him, tells his grandson that the world is divided into unprincipled winners and principled losers. The former were adept in the art of deception and the latter incapable of seeing through their clever game. The story ends with a description of Maveli's regret at his one-time adversary being worshipped in the temple at Trikkakkara.

There is K.J. Baby's powerful Malayalam novel *Mavelimanram* which tells the story of the trials and tribulations of an oppressed adivasi couple of Wynad. The adiyors' was originally a beautiful world where egalitarian and democratic values prevailed. They cleared fruits, sowed seeds, irrigated the land and reaped the fruits of their labour and shared the grain equitably. Then the upper caste men arrive and threaten them; but the adiyors refuse to yield, despite physical violence. The intruders quote their supposedly holy scriptures, citing the hoary myth about some people being born from the virat purusha's lower region and others from the head, shoulders and the loins. (Remember Purusha Sukta, an interpolation in the Rig Veda, which was allegedly a bid to legitimise the caste system and brahmin hegemony?) Still, the adivasis stand their ground. Then the clincher comes in the form of Malee, the upper caste god who weilds a blood-dripping sword. Trembling in fear at his sight, the adiyors give up.

In the hands of the oppressor migrant from the plains, religion proved a deadly weapon and has since then been instrumental in extracting the adiyors' consent for the iniquitous social order. It was a case of exploiters using the ideological state apparatus of religion to keep the exploited classes reconciled to their position; the latter were made to believe that their condition was divinely ordained. It was a means to develop false consciousness among the people and turn them into docile, unprotesting subjects.

The adiyors slave away under the tampuran who buys them and treats them as he would treat buffaloes. The tampuran barters them as he pleases and even holds the right to christen their children. These very witless royals were shamelessly servile to the British, even as the adivasis were fiercely loyal to the Raja of Pazhassi who battled the colonialists. Adiyor Kaippadan, who had been pawned for a paltry eight rupees, dared to flee from unfreedom to a land of freedom and social justice and set up an appropriately named Mavelimanram. Modeled on Maveli's kingdom, it is so unlike this tampurans' world where there are fetters even on their dreams, as Satchidanandan puts it in the preface to *Mavelimanram*. The dreams of the oppressed are stolen. And without dreams, life becomes animal. Only an individual who dreams will be able to realise freedom and equality. The authoritarian state fears those who dream and so needs persons and societies that are incapable of dreaming. Now at last the kaippadans are masters of their fate.

The Prathyaksha Raksha Daiva Sabha (Church of God's Revealed Salvation), a movement started by Poykayil Appachan for the liberation of slaves, sought to theorise subaltern history in its own way. In this history, the homeland of the indigenous communities, who are rechristened Adi Dravidas, is traced back to the Indus Valley or ancient Tamizhakam. Some songs identify the land they had ruled as the geographical territory of Kerala. They recall that among their ancestors were people proficient in arts and crafts, science, political administration and statecraft, poets and philosophers who made rich civilisational contributions before they were enslaved. Ritual renderings recall that the founder of the Sabha had spoken of the existence and eventual eclipse of the Dravidian civilisation much ahead of the archaeologists who unearthed the Indus sites. The position of the Adi Dravidas declined from that of historical glory as a result of the designs of the cunning Aryans. They were reduced to the status of slaves. The Adi Dravidas of Tamizhakam led a highly advanced social life without class and varna or caste stratification.

Was Mahabali a historical figure? There are striking similarities between Bali and Ashoka, the Mauryan emperor who ruled over North India for forty-one long years—from 273 to 232 BCE. Both Ashoka and Mahabali belonged to the shramana tradition; both rejected chaturvarnya and both earned the odium of the priestly class. Ambedkar has underscored the fact that the Mauryans were the only shudra dynasty to reach the top ruling echelons in India. Theirs was the only period of freedom and glory in Indian history. Misery was the lot of the people at other times, and there was defeat and darkness, as chaturvarnya flourished. This dynasty was also brought down by the machinations of the brahmin general, Pushyamitra Sunga, who ushered in an age of brahminical revivalism.

Maharashtra's Baliraja

The Bali myth runs deep in subaltern social memory outside Kerala too. In the Maratha region, Maveli of the Malayali is Bali or Baliraja. No one realised and utilised the mobilising power and emancipatory potential of the Bali myth more than

Jotirao Govindrao Phule (1827–90), the iconic crusader against oppressive brahminism who founded the Satyashodhak Samaj (Society for the Seekers of Truth). As Phule saw it, Baliraja was the original king of Maharashtra and along with Khandoba, Jotiba, Naikba and other popular gods as his aides, ruled over a casteless land.

In his classic work *Gulamgiri*, Phule strives to decimate the cultural matrix of brahminism. He championed gender equality too. The rakshasas and asuras were the heroes of the people, while Vamana was the archetype of the cunning brahmin. Phule demanded that Hindustan be rechristened 'Balistan', after the asura ruler. The Malayali has come pretty close to fulfilling Phule's demand. While the people of the North invoke Ram Rajya, Keralites fantasise about Mavelinadu where an egalitarian society is believed to have flourished. Mavelinadu is Kerala's Begumpura or City without Sorrow, envisaged by bhakti radical Sant Ravidas. There are no taxes or harassment in Begumpura, which is classless and casteless and is an urban center unlike the utopian rural Ram Rajya of Gandhi's dreams.

Phule historicised the avatar mythology and argued that the Aryans were conquerors and the much-hailed incarnations of Vishnu represented various stages in the Aryan invasion of India. He rubbished the puranic story about Vamana trampling down Bali to the netherworld. Phule's version is, well, down to earth: Vamana was the precursor to the so many colonial powers who conquered and left deep scars on the cultural, social and economic life in India. According to Phule, Baliraja's kingdom included Maharashtra, parts of the Konkan and the Malwal regions and some near Lanka. A shudratishudra ruler, Bali led the original inhabitants of India, the Dravidians. 'Vamana was the chief leader of the Vipras. He was a greedy, reckless and obstinate man. He did not at all like the growing power of Bali. So, in order to win his kingdom, he secretly collected a big army and approached the borders of Bali's kingdom... Vamana charged into Bali's kingdom with all his force, and harassing the subjects on his way, arrived near Bali's capital. Bali had no alternative but to fight the intruder even though his armies from various parts of his kingdom had failed to arrive' (Phule 2002). At the end of a protracted battle Bali was killed. His queen Vindhyavati committed sati, while son Banasura continued to fight but was ultimately forced to flee.

The memory of the Vamana–Bali confrontation continues to haunt both brahmins and subalterns in Maharashtra. In brahmin homes Baliraja continues to be construed as evil. When Vamana came home after overthrowing Bali, his wife showed him an image of the asura king she had made with wheat flour. 'See, Bali has come here to fight you,' she joked. A livid Vamana kicked the asura monarch's idol. That is the origin of the ritual of brahmins in Maharashtra kicking grain or flour images of Bali made by their wives during Dussehra, reckons Phule. After Vamana's death, Banasura recaptured his kingdom with the help of his father's allies. When Banasura's soldiers reached their homes, the women welcomed them with lighted lamps in a tray and prayed for the re-establishment of Baliraja's kingdom. So, every year on Dussehra day shudratishudra homes see a ritual re-enactment of this episode: when men come home after their ritual worship of the shumi tree, their wives and sisters greet them with a fervent prayer: ida pida javo balika rajya yevo (Let sorrows and troubles go and Bali's kingdom come.). In Maharashtra, Bali is an exclusively subaltern icon. Spokespersons of the dalit movement in Maharashtra maintain that Vamana represented the marauding Aryans and Bali the common masses of India.

In the later sections of *Gulamgiri* Phule describes Jesus Christ as the second Baliraja, an alter ego of the peasant king. 'He [Jesus] realised that the great Almighty God, our great Father and Creator, had given us the true and holy knowledge and had granted an equal right to it. He fathomed the Divine Will—that this knowledge be shared by all alike. Therefore, he undertook the task of releasing the poor oppressed brethren from the bondage of slavery by wicked, cunning and treacherous hunters like the brahmins and strove to establish the Kingdom of God on earth. The promise of our ancient women, that one day Bali's kingdom will be established on earth once again, is realised to some extent. Millions of people became the followers of this Baliraja in Europe... All of them began to work ceaselessly for this noble task of establishing God's Kingdom on earth.' Phule's animus for the brahmins is so deep that he sees them even in Europe, as perpetrators of oppression. He says ancestors of scholars like Thomas Paine joined Baliraja's band of followers.

Phule argued that the word 'kshatriya' came from 'kshetra', meaning field or land. kshatriyas were those who worked in the field. The untouchables are those of their descendants who were hit badly by the Aryan invasion. (Did not Parashurama exterminate the kshatriyas?) Ambedkar too proposed the historical thesis that the shudras were originally kshatriyas in a three-varna system, that there was a conflict between them and the brahmins. Bali led the kshatriyas, according to Phule. As Phule saw it, the prevalence of caste made it possible for the brahmins to dominate the system, besides acting as a category in the productive process. Thus it was part of the base as also of the superstructure. Shudratishudras were to form the main agency of social revolution.

Phule's interpretation of some of the other avatars is

interesting. As per him, a large number of troops of the Aryans came to India from Iran by sea. 'They came in small canoes, which used to travel fast over the sea. That was probably why the chief of that horde came to be called 'Matsya'.' Matsya killed an asura called Shankhasura and gobbled up his kingdom. After Matsya's death came another group of boats. They traveled very slowly and hence their leader was called 'Kachcha' (tortoise). After kachcha exited the scene, there came Varaha… 'He charged like a pig and snatched victory. Probably that ridiculous name Varaha was given to him by the kshatriyas, residing in regions of such valiant warriors as Hiranyaksha and Hiranyakashipu, as a mark of their disrespect for him.'

As Phule saw them, the later avatars who led the Aryans against indigenous rulers were essentially sadistic tyrants with blood on their hands. 'Nrusimha [Narasimha] was a very greedy, cunning, deceitful, treacherous, scheming, brutal and ruthless man with a well-built and formidable physique.' His victory over Hiranyakashipu followed much plotting and bloodshed. 'Parashurama, the macho mascot, was a bully; he was an audacious, vicious and barbarous villain. He did not hesitate to behead his mother Renuka. He was burly and was a skilled archer.'

The anti-caste crusader was actively subverting the brahminical structure of ideas and beliefs so that a new, more equitable order could emerge. His is a shudratishudra rewriting of history. It is not scientific as much as it is subversive. That was its purpose: subversion and destruction. His writings on the brahminical gods and on the history of the Aryan race have to be understood in terms of their purpose. Whether the Aryans constitute a race at all, or whether they came from Iran or anywhere else, is beside the point. Phule was not writing history.

He was rewriting brahminical 'history' from a shudratishudra perspective. Surprisingly, Phule does not seem to have paid much attention to later avatars like Rama and Krishna.

In *Shivaji Pavada*, a ballad, Phule drew parallels between Shivaji and Baliraja. Like the asura king, Shivaji was a shudra ruler. It is pointed out that since Shivaji was not a kshatriya, priests in Maharashtra refused to crown him Chhatrapati. So Shivaji sent for a priest from Kashi who first performed the sacred thread ceremony and then crowned him—after extracting a handsome amount for performing the ritual. If Baliraja was cheated of his power by the crafty Vamana, Shivaji's descendants suffered at the hands of the cunning Peshwa brahmin rulers.

For several mass movements in Maharashtra, Baliraja was an icon. In late last century Sharad Joshi of the Shetkari Sanghatana, the farmers' organisation from Maharashtra, identified Baliraja's kingdom with sustainable development which meant producing items that will fulfill people's needs, keeping intact the foundations of production. Peasants in southern Maharashtra built a 'Baliraja Memorial Dam' in 1990. The 1989 Nanded conference of the Shetkari Sanghatana was hopeful that troubles and sorrows will go and the kingdom of Bali will come. The Sanghatana pitted the exploited in the villages against the exploiters in the cities, agriculture-centered development against development based on heavy industry. Writer Gail Omvedt and friends even launched a 'Baliraja cultural movement' to prepare the cultural ground for a pan-India struggle against socio-economic exploitation.

4

Mahabali's Tribe

MAHABALI was an asura. But who were the asuras? Who were the rakshasas and rakshasis (ogres and ogresses)? In the puranas those described in these terms were often stereotyped as wicked creatures with ugly features. We are asked to look at them as the necessary antagonistic element to the 'good' represented by the protagonists of brahminical Hinduism. This falls comfortably within the age-old archetypal binary we have come to expect from mythology. But this simplicity hides a history of colonisation and the stigmatisation of particular peoples by the crusading force of an unjust aggressor.

Mythologically, the devas and asuras were children of Prajapati Kashyapa, the creator and preserver god of Vedic literature—devas by Aditi and asuras by the other spouse, Diti. Friction brewed between the asuras and devas from childhood and it only grew with time. Prajapati had a soft corner for the devas. The relationship between the asuras and devas has been multi-layered. The Rig Veda does not consistently show the asuras and devas as sparring partners; the asuras are frequently referred to with respect. They were not simply seen as evil demons back then. Indra and Varuna, the war and sea gods respectively, were mentioned as asuras as was the dark-complexioned Krishna, who ended up as Vishnu's avatar and a preeminent god in the puranas.

Then came a relentless campaign—social, cultural, economic—drummed up on behalf of the Hindu gods against the asuras. The overjoyed devas began to shower flower petals whenever asura blood was shed. There is a story about Parashurama cracking down on the asuras, using weapons supplied by Lord Siva. Paranoia marked the conduct of the devas. They saw an asura behind every bush, behind everything that went wrong. At Chitrakoot, Rama was relaxing, his head on Sita's lap. A crow flew in and pecked at Sita's bosom and Rama thought it could be none other than an asura. He took a blade of grass, made an arrow of it and lobbed it at the bird. The bird, Kakasura, was spared only once it sought refuge at the feet of the Ayodhya prince, and even then, at the cost of one of its eyes.

In the Kurukshetra battle Bheema's son Ghatotkacha, and many other, asuras fought to the death on the side of the Pandavas. A merciless Krishna consoles the heartbroken father, saying that Ghatotkacha was an asura after all, and so the death, even if it happened to be his son's, was not worth shedding tears over.

B.R. Ambedkar is of the view that asuras and devas, rakshsas, rashasis and gandharvas were all ordinary people. It was the brahmins who had them transformed into strange creatures, investing them with unusual characteristics in order to maintain cultural domination. In the puranas, the shudra adversaries of the upper castes are shown as monstrous, fang-spouting rakshasas and asuras. From temple sculptures and murals, starting from the eighth century CE, to representation in popular comics like Amar Chitra Katha, down to blockbuster movies like *Bahubali*, such stereotypes are reinforced.

Bakasura of the Mahabharata was a byword for gluttony. The story goes that he had been terrorising the citizens of the region for a long time. The responsibility of satisfying his insatiable hunger every day was on the people in nearby villages. Worse, the asura chieftain would eat, in addition to the food, the person who took it to him. During their exile, the Pandavas lived as the guests of a poor family who lived near Asuralay village which is now in Birbhum district of West Bengal. When that family's turn came to send food to the asura, Bheema volunteered to go with the food—lest his indigent hosts lose a member. In the inevitable fight that followed, the Pandava prince killed the asura. Incidentally, recent excavations in Asuralay have unearthed an artisan village of the 2000 to 1000 BCE vintage.

The cultural icons of the backward castes include a raft of asuras who were humiliated or became martyrs—Ravana, his brother Kumbhakarna, sister Shoorpanakha and Mahishasura. The word 'rakshasa' seems to bear a close relation to 'raksha', which means protection; hence, the Dravidians began to be called rakshakas—protectors of the earth and indigenous culture. 'Rakshasa' is a corruption of 'rakshak'. Romila Thapar has noted that all those opposed to the Vedic religion, even if they were Aryans like the Buddhists and the Jains, underwent a process of rakshasisation and were dismissed pejoratively as dasyus and asuras, rakshasas and rakshasis (demons, ogres and ogresses).

In the Bhagavad Gita, Krishna attributes all vices to the rakshasas and asuras. He says rakshasas and asuras are those people in whom the rajasic and tamasic elements predominate. The devious ideology of the Gita comes out when Krishna tells Arjuna that the asuras were unable to understand the divinity in the incarnation of god in human form. The implication clearly is that those who do not accept his doctrines—materialists and heretics, atheists and agnostics, those who do not accept the Vedas—were asuras. He was targeting the Buddhists and Jainas under whose rational spell the Pandava prince had obviously come. Those asuras who have achieved atmajnan—self-awareness—are not asuras, according to Adi Sankara. Gandhi's interpretation in his treatise on the Gita is that the rakshasas and asuras are witless ones who have resorted to the delusive nature of monsters and devils.

The Aryans who came to India in groups were admittedly migrants, not conquerors. However, they faced opposition from indigenous tribes and so a long-drawn-out confrontation followed. Satapatha Brahmana admits that the asuras owned the earth at first, the devas had so much as one seated can see. The scenario changed fast and devas came to control the bulk of the land. The death of every asura icon has been connected with the Aryan influx into this land. Neo-Buddhists do not celebrate any festival which marks the death of an asura because for them the killing represented a desire to finish off the untouchables. Sankranti is not celebrated because it was a celebration of the murder of Tilasur by two sisters, Sati and Kinkranti.

The Rig Veda contains innumerable references to conflicts between the migrant Aryans and the indigenous tribes. The winners began to identify themselves in their myths as devas and the defeated as asuras. In contemporary society, it is dangerous to associate villainy with migrancy. It is equally dangerous to conservatively hold on to some pastoral dream of a past that ought to be brought back. Culture thrives on inter-mixing and multiple streams of influences. However, what is being contested is the colonising force of particular incursions into a territory. As also, the validity of certain value systems which gain dominance: whether they are just and justifiable. One must remember that migrancy doesn't happen in a neutral context, and it is the context that is paramount. The Aryans forcibly evicted people from the land they lived in and wove them into their mythology as asuras. These myths also depict asuras with several indicators that denote age, that they were a prior and more ancient entity. What is this but an indication of the fact that the Aryans violently appropriated land from its indigenous occupants? For the brahmin, the devas personified virtue and the asuras evil. There is reason to think that the bulk of today's upper castes are descendants of those who triumphed. Going by Taittiriya Brahmana, the shudratishudras are the progeny of the asuras.

Asuras in Kerala agriculture

A popular myth in Kerala has it that Annam Cherukili, a pulaya girl, brought a hundred and one varieties of paddy seeds from heaven to the province. The "Vithupattu" (seed song) sings praises of each seed variety. In the eighteenth and nineteenth centuries, the pulayans who would take land on lease from landlords would use cow dung, ash and plant leaves as manure in the paddy fields. In the popular Onappattu there is a reference to paddy cultivation and bountiful harvests. The dalit labourer nurtured and sustained agriculture and farm culture in Kerala. Duarte Barbosa, a Portugese writer and colonial officer who travelled to Kerala in the sixteenth century, specifically recorded that the pulayans lived in rickety shacks from which the upper castes kept their distance. There was severe unapproachability—to let the upper castes know about their arrival, they would make a loud noise from a distance.

The 1931 agriculture census reported that non-dalit farmers lacked the disposition and skills for agricultural work. In the 1980s the commission on the socio-economic condition of the Scheduled Castes and Scheduled Tribes observed that the dalits were the backbone of agriculture in Kerala, but they had neither the ownership of technology nor land and so stood the risk of being displaced by new innovations.

Unlike the brahmins who have had a visceral aversion for manual work, the asuras and their descendants have an indelible association with the productivity of work. In the days of the Buddha, physical toil was respected. So Buddhists, Jainas and Ajivikas earned the sobriquet 'shramanas'—shrama means physical work, and shramana is one who labours, toils. The brahminic caste system looks down upon labour: the tougher the labour, the lower one is placed in the hierarchy. The shramanas, with their radical views on life and society, were the cultural leaders of the indigenous people. Resistance to caste is part of the shramana tradition, which dates back to the age of early Jainism. The shramanas gave up their homes and roamed around in search of truth, striving hard for the welfare of the common people. Not being in search of god, they looked down upon religious rituals.

The dalits were legatees of a great culture of work and acquired work skills. These skills can be seen in agriculture and in the construction of buildings. The unfreedom of the European serf was of an anonymous, class nature, while direct producers in India faced segregated forms of 'collective unfreedom'. Toiling in squalid surroundings, the dalits created all the country's wealth. The pariah is synonymous with cultivation. 'Cheru' means mud and slush and those who toil in slushy mud are called 'cherumans' in Malayalam. It was the dalit farm workers, not the 'educated' upper caste landlords, who discovered the idea of filling the kayal (backwaters) with soil and using that land for farming in Kuttanad, a region in Kerala that has the distinction of being the only place in the world where farming happens below sea level. The songs which the pulayans popularised give a graphic account of the history of subaltern Kerala.

Human social practice is the source of all knowledge; it is our ability to be productive with the raw materials available to us that allows further thinking and abstractions: these are borne by the material progress of labour. Culture cannot be uncoupled from labour. Hard, backbreaking work is the lot of the asuras' successors. There is a great joy of work one can learn from the asuric ethos. The labouring masses are the true creators of all ideas. Etymologically, 'culture' is derived from 'cultivation'. In the hands of the rising privilegentsia, however, the meaning of 'culture' got distorted and cultural relations came to be treated as commodities, which can be exchanged for a price by those who can afford this transaction, thus effacing the role of labour.

The asuras were a casteless society and had a democratic set-up, with an elected council holding power. 'When the kings of Egypt were building great tombs to bury themselves, the democratic council of the asura kingdom was busy laying roads, building hospitals, drainage systems, and everything they thought was useful for the people,' writes Anand Neelakanthan. 'Our sense of justice differed from what the learned and privileged considered right. We decided our righteousness and defined our rights in our own way. … Our dharma was based on simple things: a man should be true to his word; he should speak from his heart; and should not do anything he considered wrong. One should not cheat, even if one was sure to fail. One should honour women and not insult anyone. If there was injustice, we had to fight at all costs.'

As early as 1924, English philologist and historian, H.M. Chadwick, sought to identify asuras of the Indo-Iranian mythology with the Assyrians. Chadwick suggested that 'asura' was derived from Asur, which is what the Assyrians were called. According to A.L. Basham, author of the classic work *The Wonder That Was India* (1954), in Persia Zoroaster adopted the term asura as part of the title of the great god of light, Ahura Mazda.

N.V. Krishna Warrier too argued that the asuras originally belonged to Assyria from where one of the streams of Dravidian migrants is known to have come to India. Warrier maintained that the asuras were legatees of the great Mesopotamian civilisation. Either Mahabali was a king in Nineveh in the Assyrian region or he represented the royal throne over three thousand years ago. The subjects of that Dravidian king must have celebrated what is now Onam in his honour and brought the festival with them into southern India, via the Indus region. The Assyrians were specialists in geometry and their deities were shaped like towers with a quadrilateral base. Like the pyramids of Egypt, the trikkakkarappans that spring up in courtyards in Kerala during the four days beginning with Thiruvonam resemble these Assyrian deities. However, K.T. Ravivarma, who penned a sweeping tour de horizon covering the Bali–Vamana literature and the celebrations around the country, does not agree with Warrier (Ravivarma 2001). Ravivarma is of the view that Bali is very much an Indian icon and the Bali–Vamana myth has evolved down the ages.

The agaria asurs, to give their full name, were believed to be enemies of the Aryans. Verrier Elwin thought the agarias and the asuras were the descendants of a tribe which is represented by the Asura of Sanskrit literature and the traditions of present day asur tribe on the hills of the borderland of Ranchi, Jashpur and Palamu appeared to connect them with the Asura of Hindu mythology. There is an eight-thousand-strong asura tribe in West Bengal.

The ten-headed asura

The ten-headed king of Lanka who spirited away Sita from the forest, lodged her in his palace and ultimately fell to Rama's arrows in the war that followed is the most outstanding asura, after Mahabali. We saw that Rama who is considered an avatar of Lord Vishnu is hardly worshipped in Kerala. There are vast regions in central and north India where not only is Dasharatha's eldest son not worshipped, but his bête noire is a hero for large sections of the Adivasi population, a revered mascot in many a subaltern eye. The historical consciousness of many groups in Bengal, Jharkhand, Uttar Pradesh, Madhya Pradesh, Himachal Pradesh and Maharashtra makes them revere Ravana. Hailed as Lankesh and Dasanana, Ravana was the son of Vishravas, a brahmin holy man, and an ordinary tribal woman. He was born in Bisrakh in what's today called Gautam Buddh Nagar, some twenty kilometres from Delhi. 'Bisrakh' is believed to be an adaptation of 'Vishravas'. Saivites believe that Ravana was an ardent devotee of Lord Siva. Quite a few stone Siva lingas and idols, besides a badly damaged Nandi bull, have been recovered from the village which, it is believed, was a great centre of Saivism. The Lanka ruler who ended up as a tragic figure had two brothers—Kumbhakarna and Vibheeshana and a sister—Shurpanakha. Their father bequeathed all his wealth to Kubera, their step-brother who, consequently, came to possess unlimited wealth. Ravana and his brothers were left with nothing. Yet

Ravana did not deviate from the path of righteousness.

Killing Ravana was Rama's mission. Ravana, so goes a puranic story, had wangled a boon from Brahma that no god, asura or rakshasa will be able to kill him. Unfortunately he omitted to mention humans who, he thought, were too weak to be of any match to him. The clever Vishnu incarnated in Ayodhya as the son of Dasaratha and Kausalya to fulfil his unholy duty of murdering Ravana.

Ravana's marriage with Mandodari, the vivacious daughter of Maya, the master architect who built the fantasy palace of the Pandavas, was solemnised in Mandore in Jodhpur. One of the five perfect women in the world, folklore has it that Mandodari ran into Ravana when the asura king was in the forest hunting. Her aged father was looking for a groom for Mandodari and Ravana offered to marry her. Some of his relatives stayed back after the marriage and so people in Mandore claim asuric lineage. In 2005, a statue of Ravana was installed in Mandore.

Dasanana was head and shoulders above his Aryan adversary. He was a polymath and even his enemies recognised his versatility and erudition. On the asura king's death, Rama is said to have told his brother Lakshmana that Ravana was a learned man, a great king from whom one could learn the art of governance. Ravana was well-versed in the Vedas, Smritis and music. This ardent devotee of Lord Siva authored Shivatandava Stuti, besides a book on astrology. A known connoisseur of music, he was a virtuoso veena player and devised a musical instrument. It is believed that while praying to Siva, Ravana took a nerve from his hand, stretched it and played on it to please the lord. The single-stringed fiddle came to be known as ravanhattha veena, the present 'ravanahastha'. It consists of a bamboo stick and a coconut shell resonator and produces a wholesome sound and finds mention in ancient books on music. He was a master of the Siddha system of medicine and had acquired expertise in making Ayurvedic medicines, even using otherwise lethal chemicals like mercury. Ravana penned books on pulse diagnosis and preparation of medicines by distillation. He was also familiar with the art of embroidery and astrology. The chausar game was the brainchild of Ravana who devised it on learning that his spouse was getting bored. The two would play the game and Ravana would see to it that Mandodari always won. Ravana gave the asuras dignity and self-confidence.

Tamil brahmins used Max Mueller's concept of the cultural superiority of Aryans to legitimise their authority, while those who launched the Dravidian movement opposed this vehemently. The Dravidian movement offered a sharp critique of Ramayana which, Periyar E.V. Ramasamy argued, was the story of the subjugation of the indigenous Dravidians by the invading Aryans. He attempted an iconoclastic reading of the epic in which Ravana replaced Rama as hero. Periyar even asked Tamils to burn the Hindu epic to counter the destruction of the effigies of this kaleidoscopic personality and his brother and son in North India. This angered the orthodox brahmins and in August 1956 he was arrested while on his way to the Marina Beach in Madras to publicly burn Rama's pictures. In numerous public meetings Dravidian activists burnt the Ramayana for its portrayal of Dravidians as rakshasas or at best as monkeys and bears who were allied to Rama. Dravida Kazhakam activist and film personality M.R. Radha's theatrically provocative parody of the Ramayana depicts Ravana as a great icon. P. Sundaram Pillai, a nineteenth century Indian researcher, also praised Ravana for his virtues and said Rama was the leader of the invading Aryans. There are tomes like *Ravana the Great: King of Lanka* by M.S. Purnalingam Pillai and *Ravana Kaviyam*, an epic reconstruction of the puranic story by Pulavar Kulantai. *Ravana Kaviyam* was first published in 1946, but two years later the Congress government banned the work. Only in 1971 when the Dravida Munnetra Kazhagam came to power was the ban removed.

In the puranas there is Hiranyakashipu, the asura whose son Prahlada is a pious Vishnu devotee, and is devoured by the lord's Narasimha avatar. As part of the Dravidian movement's mission of producing counter-puranas, the poet, Bharatidasan, wrote the play *Iraniyan Allatu Inaiyarra Viran* (Hiranya or the Inimitable Hero) which was first staged in 1934.

Fiery ordeal of asuras

Religious sentiments are easily hurt in India. Derogatory comments on their 'gods' provoke in the Hindus who celebrate Dussehra to mark the victory of Rama over Ravana much anger and violence. A few years ago, Mahesh Chandra Guru, a professor in the department of communications and journalism at the University of Mysore, was jailed and suspended from his post for using 'derogatory language' in describing the hero of Ramayana. Meanwhile, in several parts of the Hindi heartland Dussehra concludes, with great fanfare, with the burning of the effigies of the ten-headed monarch and his brothers, who are held in high esteem in other parts of the country. The cacophonous ritual which causes a lot of avoidable air and noise pollution is said to mark the defeat and death of Ravana and symbolise the triumph of good over evil. Shouldn't the same yardstick of 'hurt sentiments' and 'derogatory actions' also apply to these groups who desecrate without compunction the image of a figure that is divine to a large number of groups in India?

The Bharatiya Dalit Panther Party (BDPP) raised its voice against the burning of effigies of Lord Ravana. The party wanted the government to ensure that asura icons are accorded due respect. In Pokhrayan in Kanpur Dehat district of Uttar Pradesh, the BDPP organised a mela to protest the effigy burning. The Ravana dahan has for long been a festering wound in the hearts of the gonds of central India, a proto-Dravidian tribe, the second largest tribe in the country. The gonds believe that Ravana was their king. They deny being Hindus and also dispute the conventional idea about the geographical location of Ravana's Lanka. Lanka lay in the Amarkantak mountain region of Madhya Pradesh, they say, not in the Indian Ocean. In Gondi, 'Lanka' denotes a hilly place. The gonds believe that Brahma created Ravana as a member of their tribe, for the protection of the environment. For them, Rama was an antagonistic figure who came to the rescue of the yajna-obsessed brahmin holy men whose rituals involving fire polluted the air and disturbed peace and tranquillity in the homeland of the non-Aryan adivasis. The asuras protested against the sacrifice of animals in the yajnas conducted by the brahmins and earned their wrath. Here Ravana is an anti-god, a counter to Aryan god Rama who killed a Dravidian for daring to learn the Vedas. The Gondwana Gond Samskriti Bachao Samiti was born in 1991, at the height of the Ram Janmabhoomi movement.

In July 2017 the Supreme Court heard a petition seeking an end to the burning of Ravana and other asuras. The petitioner argued that there was no mention of the burning ritual in the Ramayana of Valmiki or Tulsidas. It was all a matter of faith, ruled the apex court and dismissed the petition. Yet, the demand for a ban on the destruction of the asura effigies persists. There have been processions, prayer meetings, memoranda to authorities.

In the town of Baijnath in Himachal Pradesh, which boasts of a thirteenth century Siva temple, residents do not celebrate Dussehra. It is believed that the ancient temple was established in the town only thanks to Ravana.

For several adivasi tribes, the burning of Ravana effigies is a source of hurt and a reminder of a history of oppression. In the 1970s, a gondi language scholar based in Nagpur, Motiram Kangale, launched a movement demanding an end to Ravana's fiery ordeal. The agitators sought legal recourse but nothing substantial came of the campaign. The gonds have worshipped Ravana for ages. The burning of Ravana effigies started only in 1833 on Raja Bakshi Maidan in Nagpur, according to Kangale. The agitation was a turning point in Kangale's life, one that has defined his identity ever since. A journalist teased him about his first name Motiram and he changed his name. He is now 'Motiravan Kangale'. While on the subject of names, the youth who founded the radical dalit organisation Bhim Sena in Uttar Pradesh calls himself Chandrashekhar Azad 'Ravan'. A UP minister touched off a stir when he dubbed Samajwadi Party chief Mulayam Singh Yadav to Ravana and Mayawati of the Bahujan Samaj Party to Shoorpanakha, the asura titan's insulted sister. Acting on a complaint by a citizen, the Election Commission registered a case. The media described the comments as 'derogatory', but not everyone considered them so. In universities in Andhra Pradesh, history and mythology are being re-read. During Dussehra the students commemorate Ravana's death.

Raj Kumar Atikaye, president of the Punjab Safai Karmachari Welfare Board, says that there is a need to follow Ravana's ideals. True, the Lanka king abducted Sita, but the motive was revenge, not lust. The Lanka monarch did not so much as touch her when she was under his custody. He was wreaking vengeance for the mutilation of his sister by Lakshmana. Yet, in Ravana, orthodox Hindus see a personification of lust, conceit and megalomania. Ravana is worshipped at a 125-year-old temple in the Shivala area of Kanpur. The asura king is decorated and after purification an aarti is performed. The Dashanana mandir, they say, was constructed in 1890 by king Guru Prasad Shukla in the premises of a Siva temple. His devotees worship the asura king before moving to the Siva shrine. After the burning of the Ravana effigy in the Ramlila ground in Shivala, the doors of the Dashanana mandir remain closed for a year. The temple opens its doors for devotees only on Dussehra day next year. Around fifteen-thousand faithful throng the temple. Incidentally, there is a place called Ravaneswaram in Kerala.

Ravana mahotsavs are held in several districts of Maharashtra—Gondia, Chandrapur, Bhandara, Gadchiroli and Amravati—the objective being protection of the gond culture. Ravana was the tenth dharma guru of the gonds and was carrying forward the legacy of Kupar Lingo, the supreme ancestor of the tribe. As the asura raja's image is carried on a tusker, cries of 'Jai Ravana Raja' go up in the air. In Salher in Nasik district the adivasis see their protector in Ravana.

The year 2016 saw a clash between residents of Bisrakh in Gautam Buddha Nagar, off Delhi, who were proud of their Ravana ancestry and were all set to install an image of the asura monarch in a newly built temple, and members of a few Hindu fundamentalist organisations. Cow protection vigilantes ransacked the shrine and vandalised the statue leading to police intervention. In Shivalal and in Ravan village of Madhya Pradesh, Kanyakubja brahmins worship Ravana who, they believe, belonged to their brahmin sub-sect. In this village the blessings of Lankesh are sought on every solemn occasion.

A.K. Ramanujam, author of *Three Hundred Ramayanas*, says the feeling one gets from Jain texts is that Ravana was a noble hero. According to fifth century Jain scholar Vimalasuri, who rejected the brahminical version of the Rama story, the rakshasas were not demons, nor vanaras (monkeys). They were Vidyadhars, men and women endowed with extraordinary vidya (knowledge). In his work Paumachariyam (Patmacharitram), Vimalasuri portrays Ravana as a learned and noble devotee of Jaina masters; he acquired his magical powers through austerities and belonged to the Meghavahana clan which is linked to the Chedis who find mention in the Vedas. In Paumachariyam, Gautama, a disciple of Mahavira, tells king Seniya (Srenika) that Ravana was a great ruler and a devout Jaina, one of the sixty-three mahapurushas. Here Ravana has only one head—the nine others are reflections from the large gemstones in the necklace he wears. Another interpretation is that the ten heads represented his multifarious intellect. In some Jain texts Sita is Ravana's daughter.

Some of the Jain Ramayanas commend Ravana for his noble character and control over passions, which are worthy of a sage. He is described as a great ruler, well-read and cultured. In the Jain Ramayana by Hemacandra (1089–1172), Ravana is shown as a man of high discipline—meditating in the dense forest, serene and single-minded. Forest spirits (yakshas) transform themselves into seductive damsels and then into terrifying jackals and serpents, but he is neither tempted nor frightened. In the fourth century CE text, Lankavatara Sutra, we see the responsible ruler of Lanka listening attentively to the Buddha's discourse and inviting him to visit his island country.

Mahishasura

People in vast swathes of land spread over Uttar Pradesh, Jharkhand, Bihar, Orissa, West Bengal and Karnataka believe that Mahishasura, who was half-asura, half-buffalo, was an incarnation of Mahabali, and like Bali, a metaphor for virtuous kingship, equality and justice. He is believed to have conquered heaven and earth, and driven the gods out of their turf and earned the sobriquet of being the most powerful personage in the universe. The devas feared that if he lived for long, human beings would stop worshipping them. So they plotted against him. He put up a brave fight against the invading Aryans. But the Aryans sent Durga to finish him off. She could kill the chivalrous tribal chieftain because he would not take up arms against women, the aged and the physically weak. They say all asura tribesmen were burnt except for one sick man thanks to whom the tribe managed to avert extinction.

Many adivasi areas have seen a cultural invasion by the brahminical elite. During the nine-day puja festival, people in Bengal celebrate the victory of goddess Durga over Mahishasura. The adivasis, however, worship the martyr, not the assassin. They dismiss with contempt the mainstream Hindu narrative and during the Durga Puja mourn the death of the asura who, they believe, was their ancestor but is pictured as buffalo-headed. The counter-narrative claims that Mahishasura was a Buddhist ruler. Himself a great scholar, he hosted lectures and sermons by other scholars and upheld human values. This was intolerable to the brahminical Hindus and for them he became an embodiment of evil and wickedness. Mahishasura hit the headlines in 2011 when a section of the students of the Jawaharlal Nehru University in Delhi commemorated the martyrdom of the antigod. Aficionados of the asura icon in JNU brought out a pamphlet which allegedly cast aspersions on the goddess who is supposed to have killed the asura god. This university had a sizable representation of students from the interiors of West Bengal, UP, Jharkhand and other North Indian states where the people do not subscribe to conventional Hinduism.

In 2014, JNU saw a clash between supporters of Mahishasura, and the sura-worshippers. The Sangh parivar mouthpiece *Panchajanya* produced a scolding polemic against the prayers to Lord Mahishasura that were being conducted in JNU. In Parliament, Smriti Irani, the then minister for human resource development in Narendra Modi's cabinet, waxed eloquent on the alleged irreverence of JNU students. She delivered a fiery speech in which she castigated the students for circulating a pamphlet lauding Mahishasura and lambasting Durga. Incidentally, she reeled out a series of non-facts and presented them as facts and consequently attracted a privilege motion. This was after the suicide of dalit research scholar Rohith Vemula in Central University of Hyderabad and the arrest of Kanhaiya Kumar, president of the JNU Students' Union.

The All India Backward Students' Forum alleges that the observance of Mahishasura's martyrdom is part of an effort to free subalterns from brahminical ideological fetters. There does not seem to be anything religious about the mourning. It is also said that Mahishasura was the clan leader of tribals in the santhal region. In some parts of West Bengal during Dussehra men and women belonging to the eight-thousand-strong agricultural asura tribe avoid the vicinity of Durga puja pandals which, in their eyes, represent the wrongs done to the great king. During the five days of puja, santhals in UP lock themselves in and keep off daylight. Everything that has to be done during day is done after sunset. The asur tribe of Jharkhand with a population of ten-thousand is classified as a 'particularly vulnerable tribal group' by the Indian government with their language—spoken by some seven-thousand individuals—designated by the UNESCO as 'definitely endangered', claims ancestry from Mahishasura himself. They believe that the Devi Mahatmya story of the Markandeya Purana, which describes the birth of Durga and her nine-day long battle with Mahishasura, is biased. According to the asurs, the birth of Durga from the conjoined powers of Brahma, Vishnu and Siva was a conspiracy hatched to bring down their king who was blessed with a boon by Brahma that no man or god could kill him. Hence, the more traditionally inclined members of the asurs sometimes isolate themselves and mourn Mahishasura's death during the period of the Durga Puja.

Mahishasura was a revered figure among the adivasis of West Bengal, parts of Odisha and Jharkhand. There are people who believe he was not a mythical character but an historical figure who resisted the Aryans in the years before Christ. Recently, santhals in Bengal were up in arms when the organisers of Durga Puja in a part of Kolkata got Mahishasura made in the image of Gurmeet Ram Rahim, the notorious godman who is now languishing in jail. Ram Rahim, who is head of the Dera Sacha Sauda of Haryana, was convicted of rape.

Mahesh Chandra Guru, the aforementioned professor in the University of Mysore who was arrested for his critique of the Ramayana, believes that Mahishasura was a Buddhist king of Mahisha Mandala. The priestly class projected him as an 'asura'. He symbolised equality and justice and people who didn't tolerate his popularity conspired and manufactured stories to project him as a demon. Folklore expert Kalegowda Nagavara thinks Mahishasura who ruled Mysuru was a good administrator. A massive statue of Mahishasura was installed at the entrance of Chamundi Hills in Mysore during Chikkadevaraja Wadiyar's time.

Narakasura

Students of Osmania and Kakatiya Universities sing songs in praise of the martyr monarch who is said to have ruled over a vast kingdom. There are people who believe Narakasura possessed divine powers and treated sick children. On Diwali day, dalit and adivasi students mourn the death of Narakasura, believed to be a great Dravidian emperor who ruled over a vast kingdom. He was a nature lover who had fallen to the designs of the invading Aryans. Adivasis in Karimnagar and Khammam districts worship Narakasura. Needless to say, in brahminical mythology, Narakasura was a terrible demon, and was 'heroically' brought down by Krishna.

5

People's Gods and Goddesses

THE MULTIPLICITY of religious traditions obtaining in Kerala differs from the hegemonic sanatan Hinduism in two important respects. First, the rituals and liturgical rites observed in Kerala have not been influenced by those of the Aryavrata tradition and are observably separate. And second, the mythologies peddled by Hinduism don't have much import on the Malayali consciousness—here myths inhabit an entirely different universe if not sit in complete opposition to their Aryan counterparts. The state sees a profusion of non-Aryan gods that are nowhere to be found in the sanatan schema.

For instance, the premier deity of puranic Hinduism, the Ayodhyan prince Rama, is hardly ever worshipped. This, in the land of Adi Sankaracharya, the darling son of 'inclusion'-minded brahminism. Nor do people in Kerala celebrate Diwali, a festival in memory of the triumph of Rama, Sita and Lakshmana over the asura king, Ravana, and their subsequent homecoming after fourteen years in exile. Small wonder, Malayalis, barring the Sangh parivar faithful, are not excited about the construction of a Rama temple in Ayodhya. The hindutvavadi attempt to unite Indians under the banner of 'reclaiming' the legacy of Rama doesn't hold much water in Kerala.

Krishna, no doubt, is widely worshipped and is the main deity in famous temples like those in Ambalappuzha and Guruvayur. However, to begin with, he was an asura, an adivasi clan leader, and an opponent of the Aryans who even confronted Indra. The apotheosis of Krishna is a later development. Deified as an avatar of Lord Vishnu, his violent advice to Arjuna in the Bhagavad Gita came to be regarded as the central text in the Hindu canon. Kerala also hasn't fetishised or worshipped the cow as has happened in other states. The sizeable Muslim, Christian and avarna populations of the state cook and consume all manner of meat and sea food with great delight. So there is no ban on cow slaughter unlike in the North. In fact, some of the indigenous deities worshipped in Kerala are believed to relish meat, not excluding beef, a practice that would be anathema to followers of mainstream Hinduism.

Kerala boasts of a fascinating and diverse spiritual heritage. The galaxy of deities worshipped include anti-gods, anti-heroes, mother goddesses, and holy men of Mahayana Buddhism and Jainism, all figures classical Hinduism loves to hate. Also prevalent is the practice of ancestor worship. The bulk of the gods and goddesses worshipped in the state are too non-Aryan to fit into the Hindu pantheon. So it isn't surprising that several attempts to dismantle this subaltern regime of worship have been attempted in Kerala, with some success.

In non-Aryan forms of spirituality and worship, devotees have 'direct access' to the divine. The kind of mystique that surrounds the Hindu deities and their sanctum sanctorum is happily absent in still existent prelapsarian shrines that serve dalit devotees. There is no professional priest—often the tribal chief or a community elder officiates. The relationship between the worshipper and the worshipped is personal, informal, intimate. Meat, cigar and liquor are often part of the religious proceedings and are not taboo objects—often these are presented as offerings to deities like Chathan, ancestor Mutthappans and mother goddesses like Kali and Kurumba whom some irreverently call non-vegetarian gods.

Hinduism, on the other hand, thrives on the colonisation of other faiths. To cite just one case, journalist Saba Naqvi reported in 2013 of the efforts to divest some Sufi shrines in Maharashtra of their Islamic identity for inclusion into the Hindu pantheon.

Linguist Gopalakrishnan Naduvattam presumes that upon being disallowed from setting up temples, people belonging to the lower castes built places of worship of their own. Dalit gods form a long cavalcade of victims of class violence and caste tyranny and champions of lost causes. They fought upper caste domination and socio-economic inequalities. Their protruding teeth and weapons suggest the anger of the marginalised people and their readiness to fight the exploiters. Animal sacrifice and common dining are some of the features of folk worship, which is not governed by any 'holy' texts. Some folk deities serve as unifying forces as they are worshipped by people belonging to various castes and even religions. To cite some cases, Christians, Muslims and Hindus worship Ayyappa, as we will see, and minor gods in kavus.

An example of a folk deity who was later appropriated by an insurgent brahminism was the goddess of war, Kottavai. Said to be an antecedent of Kali and Bhadrakali, this fierce goddess delighted in war. With her necklace of tiger teeth, astride a tiger, Kottavai emerged during battle to drink the blood of her foes and eat their flesh. She was birthed in the milieu of the ancient belief that the human and the divine came closest to each other in the midst of the violence of battle. Kottavai also stood for the feminine element of battle. Unlike what is believed now, war wasn't merely a domain of masculinity. Male warriors were also accompanied by female dancers, singers, drum-beaters, poets, sword enchantresses and oracles. They harnessed the demonic powers of Kottavai and other female spirits and at the end of the battle performed rituals which involved cooking the bodies of the fallen opponents. Kottavai was worshipped in tribal Kerala, in Tamizhakam, in the Sangam era, and even by the Cheras.

The places of worship of the adivasis have scarcely any resemblance to the massive Hindu temples with their elaborate architecture. Gods are found nestling under a tree, or simply in an open area, without any walled enclosure prohibiting direct contact. Such observances reflect a close relationship with the natural world and often vary depending on the mode of production and the relationship of the laity with the environment.

Among the folk deities are individuals who were either murdered or who committed suicide. People believe that the dead and the gone and the killed would visit them when needed. The banyan tree is also widely worshipped among disparate groups who do not conceive of god as a being who rules over everything. Rather, divinity is scattered across all the small things in life that people often interact with—a rock that doubles up as a seat; a coconut tree before it is climbed, the sword and armour; the waist thread—the material presence of the Thing-beyond-words.

The ancient Parabrahmam temple in Oachira in South Kerala is unique in its own way. Parabrahmam being Universal Consciousness, there is neither a covered structure nor a sanctum sanctorum. Attached to the Edappara Maladevar Nada temple near Kozhenchery is the shrine of a nineteenth century

Robin-Hood-like figure Kayamkulam Kochunny. Kochunny became an outlaw at a young age, and is said to have stolen from the rich and given to the poor. The rich included, of course, large temples which hoarded massive amounts of wealth. He was jailed for his exploits and is believed to have died in prison. There are alternate accounts of what happened to him, some say he escaped from prison, and lived a full life. Regardless, he became a symbol for the righteous vengeance of the oppressed castes. The Kochunny Nada in Patthanamthitta district has an Islamic touch, with a tomb-like structure painted in green. The unconventional offerings made by the devout include tobacco, betel leaves, incense sticks, candles, liquor and marijuana.

Another case of what may be ancestor worship, or affection for an anti-hero, is the deification of Suyodhana, the eldest Kaurava prince whom his enemies called Duryodhana. Suyodhana occupies a high pedestal in subaltern yore. He is the presiding deity in a temple in Shastankotta in southern Kerala. In the Kurukshetra battlefield, Bheema fatally wounded the Kaurava prince by hitting him on the thigh. This was done on Krishna's advice and was a clear violation of the ethics of battle. The traditional owners of the shrine believe that the place was once visited by Suyodhana, whom they fondly call Malanada Appooppan, the grandfather of the hills. There is a subsidiary shrine of Gandhari, Suyodhana's mother who lost all her one hundred sons in the war with the Pandavas. Rituals in this temple are performed by members of the Kuruva community and the offerings include toddy, arrack and chicken. A dalit shrine, the Malanadu temple attracts non-dalits too. Over the decades the Suyodhana temple has adopted a number of Hindu customs and practices.

Many sacred groves have been sucked in by Hinduism,

not only in Kerala but also in neighbouring Tamil Nadu and Karnataka. Deities made of sand and lime have been replaced by granite ones that do not dissolve in the abhishekam water. Uncovered sacred groves of mother goddesses have been Aryanised and have become Hindu kshetrams of Kali, Durga or Bhagavati, with their upper caste priests and tantris. In the case of Mandamullathil kavu in Thalassery, a savarna astrologer spread his cowrie shells and 'discovered' that the grove was situated at a place where once stood a temple. He recommended conversion of the kavu into a temple with an installed deity and daily puja. Now a board in front of the shrine announces that it is the Sree Mandamullathil kshetram. A brahmin priest performs puja. The kavu can now be mistaken for a prosperous Hindu shrine, with a big concrete hundi.

The worldly wise at the helm of devaswam affairs realise the need to move with the times and so they do not ignore the demands of the market. There are arrangements to conduct weddings, rooms where the bride and the groom can dress up and a platform on which marriages are solemnised, besides the inevitable dining hall. In Kuttikkol in North Malabar, the word 'Om' is inscribed at the gate of the kavu which used to greet every one regardless of caste or religion till recently. Boards tell 'non-Hindus' to keep off the shrines, thus demolishing a secular, cultural legacy.

The non-Aryan religious tradition has given much elegant poetry to Malayalam, besides an identity to Kerala. More mother goddesses are worshipped in Kerala than in any other South Indian state. Fiercely independent, the Dravidian mother goddess epitomises nature. Invariably associated with the non-Aryan mother deity is the oracle—velichappadu or komaram in Malayalam—who, possessed by the goddess, swoons and goes into noisy paroxysms of ecstasy. As devotees stand with folded hands, the oracle communicates with them on behalf of the goddess, and offers them solace from their private griefs. Richard Lennoy (1974) gives a vivid description of the oracle: 'In the context of the Hindu village festival the holy men whose job it is to focus the dispersed energies of the society in sacred rites may be divided into two classes of specialists: priests and oracles. The priest offers to the gods the gifts of the community as a whole; in turn, the gods enter the body of the oracle—take possession of him or her—and direct community affairs through their chosen mouthpiece. Priests, even if not invariably Brahmans, are always of a higher caste than oracles.'

Lennoy recalls the Joan of Arc story and dwells at length on the oracle's place in the caste hierarchy. 'In India, as elsewhere, the occult power of the oracle is a direct result of his vulnerable position in the hierarchic order. He is either a member of the unprivileged castes or tribes, or, as often happens, he is an aberrant personality who is innately disposed to venture into the disordered regions of the mind… Like Joan of Arc—a truly representative figure of the European Antipodes—who heard voices in the woods and was endowed by legend with ancient magical powers over animals, men, plants, and fruits, the Hindu oracle is spokesman for the submerged, inchoate, mute, and primitive forces in opposition to Brahmin authority. But unlike medieval Europe, where direct confrontation ended in ruthless suppression of the Antipodes, village India fosters cooperation between the two domains. Besides violence, ritual possession is the Hindu's prime means for canalising aggression and voicing of social protest. Through the oracle those who have suffered unjust treatment speak up and demand redress' (1974, 201).

Oracles, both men and women, are visible all over the

Kurumba temple in Kodungallur in central Kerala on Bharani day in the month of Meenam (March–April). Hundreds of oracles, wearing belts and anklets, ritual swords in hands, turmeric paste on foreheads, dance around the shrine, belting out delightfully profane verses. In divine frenzy some of them cut their foreheads and blood oozes from the wounds. Goddess Kurumba is said to love the raunchy songs sung by her devotees. The concept of the 'morally clean' goddess is challenged here as also the idea of 'decent' language.

Kodungallur was once Muziris, the capital of the Cheras, who used to have a Kali kavu where the form of worship was far from brahminical. Some historians believe that the Kurumba temple was once a Buddhist shrine, that the vulgar songs were part of a mean strategy adopted by the upper castes to drive away the Buddhists and usurp their nunnery. Gopalakrishnan Naduvattom questions this view; he says the raunchy songs and dance are a legacy of tantric Buddhism. Others think the shrine was originally linked to the agricultural fertility cult. It is also possible that in the wake of Aryanisation, the dalit devotees of the mother goddess were forced to leave Kodungallur and they were permitted to worship the goddess only on Bharani day in Meenam. Almost a century ago, in 1927, Sahodaran Ayyappan, a radical disciple of Narayana Guru, led a campaign against the singing of obscene songs and the ritual killing of roosters, which were supposed to please the goddess. The devotees present at the temple tried to manhandle him and his followers, who were then saved by the police.

Another theory links Kudumba to Kannagi, heroine of the classic Cilappathikaram ("The Jeweled Anklet"). This early Tamil classic authored by the third century Jain prince, Ilango Adigal, narrates a story of love, betrayal and vengeance.

Kannagi's husband Kovalan has to suffer the wrath of the Pandya king: he is implicated in the theft of the queen's anklet, and the kinghas him beheaded without trial. An apoplectic Kannagi—despite his affair with the courtesan Madhavi—proves her husband's innocence before the king and has the city of Madurai go up in flames. Elsewhere in South India, there are shrines of Kannagi who is said to epitomise Dravidian valour and righteousness. The Kannagi story is chanted in emotional tones before the Ponkala festival in the shrine of the mother goddess in Attukal near Thiruvananthapuram.

The ubiquitous natural kavus (sacred groves) have a tenuous connection with organised religion. In some unpretentious family shrines you will look in vain for a deity, a lamp will beckon you from the sanctum sanctorum. The trees in the sacred grove in Iringole in Ernakulam district are treated as sub-deities of Vana Durga. A number of sacred sites where local gods were worshipped maintain the ecological health of the region. Before they launched the protracted struggle for land in Muthanga, C.K. Janu and her adivasi comrades of Wayanad worshipped at the sacred groves.

Ayyappa and friends

The most popular among the gods in Kerala is Swamy Ayyappa of Sabarimala. The Sabarimala complex is located at an altitude of over four-thousand feet in the Periyar Tiger Reserve in the lap of the picturesque Western Ghats. The shrine itself is simply constructed and sits unassumingly on the banks of the Pampa in southern Kerala. During the November–January mandalam season, hundreds of thousands of pilgrims from various parts of the state, and outside, struggle up to the eighteen holy steps and from there to the abode of Ayyappa. For many devotees, the arduous trek to Sabarimala is a journey in self-discovery. The pilgrims have a collective identity. All are said belong to the same family and address one another as Swamy. Distinctions of class and caste cease to matter, though the privileged stay away from the mass event that involves rubbing shoulders and sharing with strangers. Lord Ayyappa is a Swamy too. Once a Swamy climbs the eighteen holy steps as many times, that is, undertakes eighteen pilgrimages, he becomes a 'Guru Swamy' and qualifies to guide and lead a team of pilgrims to Ayyappa's holy presence in Sabarimala.

During the 'Sabarimala season' every nook and corner of the state resonates with loud chants of 'Swamiye Sharanam Ayyappa'. The pilgrims greet one another with holy chants of 'Swamy Sharanam' or 'Ayyappa Sharanam'. Equality and austerity are essential elements of the Ayyappa cult. As a prelude to the pilgrimage, they used to undergo a rigorous process of physical and spiritual self-purification for forty-one days. The devotee is expected to lead a spartan sanyasi life, growing hair and refraining from shaving, wearing black clothes, ashes and sandal paste, abstaining from sex, meat and liquor. Braving the morning chill, he gets up early, takes a dip in a river or pond and visits a nearby temple.

The conventional belief is that Ayyappa is Hariharasuta—son of Hari (Vishnu) and Hara (Siva). He was supposedly born out of a union between Mohini, the female form of Vishnu assumed during the great churning of the primeval ocean of milk, and Siva. Mohini abandoned the child in the forest, so goes the story, and the childless ruler of Pantalam, who traces his ancestry to the Pandya dynasty of Madurai, found the infant and brought him to the palace. Ayyappa grew up in the palace where the queen later gave birth to another son. Some of the king's minions feared a likely dispute in the future over the throne. So they worked out a plan to finish off Ayyappa. On the advice of a scheming minister, the queen feigned illness and the royal physician dutifully prescribed tiger's milk. Who will bring a mother tiger or its milk from the forest? Ayyappa, brave and full of energy, volunteered to undertake the risky task. He went to the dense forest and came back astride a fierce tiger accompanied by its young ones. Will someone now milk the tiger? The palace cabal's game was up. Everyone realised that Ayyappa was divinity personified, but the young man soon bade farewell to the comforts and luxuries of the royal palace. Later, Ayyappa would go on to kill Mahishi, a she-buffalo which had been striking terror in the region.

During the British days the miniscule fiefdom of Pantalam became part of the princely state of Travancore. After the formation of the Kerala state in 1956, the shrine came under the control of the autonomous Travancore Devaswam Board which manages the bulk of the Hindu temples in southern Kerala, close to thousand-two-hundred in number, employing more than five-thousand people. There are also the Kochi and Malabar devaswam boards, besides quite a few Hindu shrines of various gods and goddesses under private ownership. The well-known Krishna temple in Guruvayur is controlled by a trust. Besides Sabarimala, numerous shrines of Ayyappa dot Kerala, but they do not insist on austerity and devotion of the kind that Sabarimala demands. While the deity in Sabarimala is a celibate, elsewhere Ayyappa is accompanied by his wife or by his consort and son.

The Hindus believe that on Ayyappa's request Parashurama, the sixth avatar of Vishnu, got the unpretentious temple constructed in Sabarimala and the celibate god was transformed into 'Dharma Sastha'. The approved mode of worship is brahminical; male brahmins alone qualify for the post of priest. Among those who look after the welfare of the pilgrims is the Sangh parivar outfit created in 1995, Ayyappa Sewa Samiti. Every six months, there is a change of melsanthi, the priest who performs the daily puja. Overseeing the ceremonies of worship is a tantri, a hereditary high priest from a brahmin family. Brahminic rituals like Ganapati homam and kalasam are performed regularly. The Sanskrit phrase "Ta Tva Masi" (Thou Art That, meaning the Self is the Absolute Reality) from Chandogya Upanishad welcomes the pilgrim to the Ayyappa's presence.

But is Ayyappa a Hindu god? He is a total stranger to North Indian Hinduism. The only puranic work in which Ayyappa finds mention is the nineteenth century *Bhoothanatopakhyanam*. He is treated as a Hindu deity although you look in vain for a god with that name in the Hindu pantheon. If he is a Hindu god, why does the Ayyappa cult remain confined to this tiny part of the country? The hill shrine is not one of the many places of worship which were built or consecrated by Aryan brahmins soon after they streamed into Kerala and around which brahmin settlements grew. The Aryan migrants from the North had settled down only in fertile planes. The touch-me-not-ism, the egregious malaise of Hinduism, is blissfully absent in Sabarimala. Unlike in some other shrines like Guruvayur, the priest here does not adopt a holier-than-thou attitude towards the devotees—he does not rush out to take a dip in an unpolluted pond or the river every time he touches a devotee accidentally. Naturally Sabarimala has not seen any Guruvayur or Vaikkam-like satyagraha by dalits stressing their right to enter the shrine or use the nearby streets. Once a person takes the vow to go to

Sabarimala and wears the ritual beads, he becomes an Ayyappa, a Swamy, himself.

The shrine has a strong plebian connection and is outside the Hindu tantric modality. 'Sabarimala', which means Sabari's hill or mountain, got the name from an adivasi woman, a character in the Ramayana. The very name 'Ayyappa' has a subaltern ring to it. Nor is the identity of his lieutenants in sub-shrines any different--Kochu Kadutha, Valiya Kadutha, Karuppa Swamy, Karuppayi Amma. In Ayyappa's holy presence Hindus, Muslims and Christians, the affluent and the indigent, stand with folded hands, shoulder to sweaty shoulder and chant a host of ecstatic 'Sharanams'—'Swamiye Sharanam Ayyappa', 'Swamy Sharanam', 'Ayyappa Sharanam'. There was a time when, the absence of caste distinctions used to keep orthodox brahmins off the shrine. It is even said that tantris had to be brought from Andhra Pradesh because Kerala brahmins did not serve in the subaltern shrine. The child wore a jewel in the neck which gave him the name 'Manikandhan'—boy with a diamond around his neck. But the adivasi community of mala arayans do not accept this theory. He is Manikandan, they say, being the son of Kandan and Karuthamma. Under his leadership the mala arayans are said to have successfully fought the Chola invaders and they began to worship him.

The Mala Arayans allege that the Tazhamon tantris grabbed the shrine from them. The name of Karimala Arayan, who was the first priest of the temple, can be found embossed on the first of the eighteen holy steps leading to the shrine, it is said. Since 1902 the tantris have been managing the puja and related matters. What followed the brahmin take-over of Sabarimala, was what, in another context, the scholar Meera Nanda dubbed 'gentrification' of the deities. There was a ritual where an adivasi priest performed 'abhishekam' on the deity with honey; it is no longer in practice. Cheerappanchira, the ezhava household at whose 'kalari' Ayyappa was trained in fighting and the use of weapons had a traditional right in the conduct of fireworks. Now the Travancore Dewaswam Board has taken the right away from the family and auctions it to the highest bidder. Nor does the family of Kadutha enjoy the rights it once enjoyed traditionally in Sabarimala. The mala arayans claim that they are legatees of a great culture, having succeeded from the Aye dynasty whose kingdom spanned from Pampa to Kanyakumari. Sabarimala was the abode of their god. The eighteen holy steps to the sanctum, they say, represent the number of hills in the region. Political parties have not shed any tears over the mala arayans' loss of their cultural capital in a state where the overall population of adivasis is less than two per cent.

The Ayyappa cult is a fascinating study in syncretism. The myth is also the story of young Ayyappa's close camaraderie with the Muslim warrior, Vavar, and the Christian priest, Veluthachan. The devotees prance and dance at a mosque in nearby Erumeli where Vavar Swamy is worshipped. The mosque is managed by the Erumeli Mahalla Muslim Jamaat, but the loud petta tullal, a dance, has all the trappings of a tribal ritual. The story goes that Ayyappa met Vavar, who was a Sufi, in far-from-friendly circumstances, but at the end of a scuffle in which neither won, they became inseparable friends. The prasadam which the priest at the Vavar palli hands over to the devotees is believed to have medicinal properties.

On their way back from Sabarimala the pilgrims break into 'sharanam' chants before the image of Fr Giacomo Fenicio at the St Andrew's Church (Basilica) at Arthunkal, a coastal hamlet near Alappuzha, leave their holy garlands there and take a dip in a nearby pond. Folklore has it that Ayyappa had a warm friendship with the Portuguese priest who was an instructor in the kalari (arms training school) in Cheerappanchira in Muhamma. Fr Fenicio who served as priest in the Arthunkal Catholic church, built by the Portuguese in the sixteenth century, was popularly known as Arthunkal Veluthachan—the white father. Veluthachan had a deep interest in indigenous culture and was also known for his healing powers. Sabarimala has thus become a byword for syncretism and a signifier of the Hindu–Muslim–Christian bond. There is also Kadutha who was another close tribal comrade of Ayyappan. By their 'sharanam' calls, pilgrims invoke all sub-deities—Malikappurath Ammaye Sharanam, Vavar Swamiye Sharanam, Kadutha Swamiye Sharanam.

Such a multi-religious association is unimaginable in a Hindu dispensation. However, the austere place is generally considered a Hindu temple. With the heavy rush of pilgrims, Sabarimala is a rich source of lucre for the Travancore Devaswam Board (TDB). The ban on the entry of women of the menstruating age to Sabarimala was formalised under rule 3(B) of the Kerala Hindu Places of Public Worship (Authorisation of Entry) Rules 1965. After the fire in 1950 and subsequent brahminisation, the recorded chant of Harivasaram in praise of Hari (Vishnu) by Yesudas, Kerala's iconic playback singer, a pious Christian and Ayyappa devotee, began to be played in Sabarimala at the end of every hectic day. It serves as a lullaby for the forest god. Thus Ayyappa is invested with a clean Hindu identity and the media dutifully laps up and repeats the claim. An attempt to Hinduise Sabarimala further was mercifully defeated in the Kerala High Court. The petitioner was T.G. Mohandas, who is credited with the discovery that the Christian church in Arthunkal was a Siva temple. Mohandas is the convener of the

Kerala BJP's intellectual cell—an indication of the intellectual capacity of the national party. There appears to be a devious plan to de-Islamise, de-Christianise, de-tribalise and de-dalitise the popular place of worship whose doors are at present open to Muslims, Christians, tribals and dalits.

The Sangh parivar is unable to digest the syncretism that is the hallmark of Sabarimala. Once there was talk of a Hindu parliament taking over the administration of the Sabarimala temple from the TDB, the obvious attraction being the crores that flow into the temple's coffers. There were media reports of Hindu pilgrims being pressured to keep off the Vavar mosque. In 1995, Hindu fundamentalists kicked up a row when Vishnu Namboodiri, the then chief priest of Sabarimala who had imbibed the spirit of the Ayyappa cult and believed that man-made religious barriers were meaningless, worshipped at the Ecumenical Church in Nilakkal. Sangh parivar ideologue P. Parameswaran fumed that by offering prayers at a non-Hindu place of worship the melsanthi had disgraced the temple and its deity. A congregation of caste organisations, with which the priest's church visit coincided, adopted a resolution asking the priest to atone for his alleged un-Hindu act.

The thousands of unshaven pilgrims trudging their way to Sabarimala do not respect barriers of caste and religion during the pilgrimage. The pilgrimage has a Buddhist flavour. Perhaps, Ayyappa was a Buddhist holy man, if not the Buddha himself. Or maybe Ayyappa and his friends were originally tribal gods who were taken over by Buddhism. It is possible that the accent on austere, sanyasi life and camaraderie and the absence of caste differences and untouchability point to the Buddhist origin of the pilgrimage to the hill shrine. Do the repeated 'sharanam' chants not ring a Buddhist bell—'Buddham Sharanam

Gachchami,' 'Dhammam Sharanam Gachchami', 'Sanghan Sharanam Gachchami'? Does the pilgrim's renunciation of the comforts of life during the pilgrimage not remind you of Gautama's own renunciation? The sitting posture of the deity in Sabarimala has striking similarities with the motif of the meditating Buddha. Ayyappa seems to be the deity of one of the many viharas and deities of Mahayana Buddhism which brahminism is known to have appropriated. Sabarimala was one of the two major Buddhist pilgrim centres in this province, the other being Sree Moolavasam near Azhikode. Established in the third century BCE, Sree Moolavasam was swallowed into the sea sometime after the ninth century. There is a view that the name 'Vavar' comes from Bavari, who was a contemporary of the Buddha and had set up a hermitage in the south, on the banks of the Godavari river.

Ayyappa is also known as Dharma Shasta. 'Dharma' (dhamma in Pali) figures prominently in the Buddhist lexicon and Shasta is another name for the Buddha. There is a relevant parallel in Buddhist religious life to the bar on adult women in Sabarimala. The Buddha had cautioned against admitting women. But one must also remember how Ananda, one of Buddha's disciples, argued against the unreason of such a rule, and convinced him to induct women into the sangha.

The bundle of puja items like a ghee-filled coconut, camphor and betel leaves which pilgrims carry to Sabarimala is 'pallikkettu'. 'Palli' is the Pali and Malayalam word for Muslim and Christian places of worship and is inextricably linked with Buddhism. 'Pallikkoodam' is Malayalam for school. While on the subject of 'palli', time was when the present Athirappilli, home to a beautiful waterfall off Thrissur, was known as Athirappalli. What took place was no innocent change in place name: with pilli supplanting palli, this place lost its shramana connection. Also, Athirappalli Sastha who inhabited the place was the god of the tribal mala vetans. Like palli, Shasta has a shramana connection as we will see. Meanwhile, the government's plan to build a hydro-electric project at great cost to the fragile ecology of the tourist spot has run into stiff opposition from the people of the state.

Another controversial aspect of the Ayyappa myth is his love story. Ayyappa's paramour Lalitha is worshipped in Sabarimala as Malikappurath Amma (Lady of Malikappuram). Malikappurath Amma is said to be waiting for the day the celibate god offers her his hand in marriage. Ayyappa had promised to marry her when—and only when—there is no first-time pilgrim. Given the increasing flow of pilgrims every year, her dream is bound to remain just that. The first-timers leave an arrow at a nearby banyan tree to register their presence. During every pilgrimage season Malikappurath Amma goes to the banyan tree, finds some arrows there and goes back disappointed. This story is bandied about as the justification for disallowing women of menstruating age from entering Sabarimala. But there are two points that need to be considered. The first is the multiplicity of the myths surrounding Ayyappa. As we have seen, there is no 'one true' myth, no canonical text, that definitively legislates the practices surrounding the Sabarimala pilgrimage. The second is the material nature of the pilgrimage itself—the very point of the ritual is that it is non-discriminatory and open to all. As times change, and society progresses and learns that those whom it defines as 'all' exclude people, correcting past mistakes to include them is but natural. The more recent rule of disallowing certain women in the temple premises, therefore, holds no water, precisely because of the egalitarian core of the Ayyappa cult. How much ever the traditionalists and brahminical groups claim otherwise, it was never their place to legislate on these matters.

There are two major pilgrimage seasons in Kerala—the mandalam season beginning in mid-November and the makaravilakku season a month later. Besides, the shrine remains open in the first ten days of every Malayalam month. The Malayali diaspora has also invented its own methods of displaying devotion to Ayyappa. Quite a few Ayyappa shrines have come up in the last few decades in every Indian city where there is a sizeable Malayali population. There is fund collection, puja is conducted and food served to the devotees in practically every locality during the mandala season.

If his early palace connection is ignored, Ayyappa is very much a subaltern god, a forest god who is shown as riding a tiger. Perhaps he was a hunter deity of the tribals. There are iconographic similarities with Ayyanar or Ayyanarappa, who is a deity mainly worshipped in villages in various parts of Tamil Nadu. The unending flow of pilgrims from the neighbouring state during every Sabarimala season may be connected with the Ayyan–Ayyappa link. Peruman and Kadaman are two other names of Ayyan, the guardian deity of villages, who protects them and their cattle from disease, ensures good rainfall and harvest. Non-brahmins serve as priests in Ayyan temples.

Going by one of the down-to-earth accounts, what we have in Sabarimala is a great martyrs' memorial and a case of hero worship. Does not the very name 'Ayyappa' have a Dravidian ring about it? This can be said about the other deities like Kadutha. Ayyappa who lived in the seventeenth century is said to have belonged to the Tamil Pandya dynasty, a section of which migrated to Kerala and settled in Pantalam. A dreaded brigand called Udayanan abducted Maya, a princess of the Pantalam palace, and her brother Rajasekharan sought the help of the Mooppan, the ezhava chief of the kalari in Cheerappanchira, to get her freed. Mooppan and his men chased the dacoit and got Maya released. Unfortunately, the royal family was reluctant to take the 'polluted' girl back and so a livid Mooppan married her off to his nephew. In 1685, Maya gave birth to a boy whom they named Ayyappa. Rajasekharan, who was childless, adopted his nephew. The young man was sent to the kalari where Lalitha, the Mooppan's daughter, had also come to learn and practise the use of weapons. During this time, Ayyappa came into conflict with Vavar, before becoming fast friends. Soon, Ayyappa and Lalitha fell in love, but before they could get married, there was another attack from a vengeful Udayanan. Vavar came to his rescue, but tragically, Ayyappa, Lalitha, Vavar and Kadutha were killed in the combat.

Another version, slightly different, which puts the year of Ayyappa's birth at some time between 860 and 865 in the Malayalam calendar (1685 and 1690 CE), says the young man did kill dacoit Udayanan, but he was later mauled by a tiger and a grief-stricken Lalitha killed herself. It is said the temple at Sabarimala was built by the ruler of Pantalam in honour of the dead Ayyappa and Lalitha; neither did he forget Vavar, his son's intimate friend. In this narrative Ayyappa and Vavar are martyrs. Over the course of time, brahminism hijacked the Ayyappa cult, which was confined to central Travancore, and gave the god a Hindu face.

In 1950, the shrine saw a fire which prompted the then chief minister of Travancore–Cochin, C. Kesavan, to comment irreverently and famously: If a temple is destroyed, that much superstition is gone. However, the temple continues to draw millions of devotees every year. Nor has superstition given way to genuine faith. To cite just one case, on Makara Sankranthi day officials of the temple, the Devaswam Board and the Kerala State Electricity Board together arrange the lighting of the Makaravilakku, in connivance with forest officials and the police for a few minutes on a nearby hill which, the gullible pilgrims are made to believe, is a natural and divine phenomenon. Millions of pilgrims turn up to witness the 'divine light'. In 2011, over a hundred pilgrims died in the melee when a stampede was set off in the rush to catch a glimpse of the Makaravilakku. For the Devaswam authorities, however, Makaravilakku is a money-spinner and they would not, despite loss of pilgrims' lives and despite protests from rationalists and atheists, discontinue the ritual.

Every government in Kerala has enthusiastically sought to promote 'religious tourism'. The bulk of those who come to Sabarimala are tourists. Quite a few of them set out for Sabarimala just for a lark or to get over their existential woes. Chief Minister Pinarayi Vijayan told the media that his government was trying to persuade the Centre to declare Sabarimala a national pilgrim centre. The astronomical hundi collection enables the Travancore Devaswam Board to keep its other temples out of the red. Shops selling puja items and black clothes have mushroomed all over the state. The multi-national Coco-Cola, which monopolised the soft drinks, drinking water and soda market in Sabarimala, made a neat pile of six crore rupees during the 2016–17 Mandala season. A transport industry consisting of taxis, vans, jeeps and auto-rickshaws, quite a few of them operating illegally, in connivance with the forest authorities and the police, thrives. Sabarimala having grown into a huge market, there is massive exploitation of pilgrims. The forest deity's abode has become an environmentally hazardous township. Already, since the early 1970s, the phenomenal pilgrim congregation has been telling badly on the environment: plastic bags and human waste foul up the region, including the supposedly sacred waters of the Pampa in which the Ayyappas are expected to take a dip before moving to the sanctum sanctorum. Non-Malayali pilgrims have a ritual of leaving their black-dyed clothes in the Pampa. The cheap dye in the clothes adds to the toxicity of the river, which is already overburdened by the thoughtless exploitation from modern industrialisation.

Challenging Adi Sankara

From Ayyappa of southern Kerala let us move to teyyam and Muttappa in the North. The word 'teyyam' is said to be a corrupted form of daivam (god). He is not the representation of god, he is god himself. It has come to represent the particular form of worshipping folk deities that is prevalent in Kerala. The songs sung to invoke the spirits of the deities are known as tottam songs. 'Tottam' is believed to be a corruption of 'stotram'. The teyyams are a political phenomenon and Pottan is the most political of them—he challenges Adi Sankara, the brahmin acharya of advaita who also belonged to Kerala. Sankara runs into Pottan, who carried a child at his waist and a pot of toddy on his head, and asks him to get out of the way to avoid distance pollution, but the organic intellectual of the dalits retorts with a simple question: 'Why do you ask me to move off?' He goes on to disabuse Sankara's mind of all notions of the latter's cultural superiority and the sanctity of the caste system:

> You smear the sandal paste
> We are bathed in dirt
> You wear the chains of gold

We wear the chain of fish...

Haven't you crossed the river in the canoe which I rowed?

The banana grown in your dump yard is the offering to your god

The basil flower grown in our dump yard is the garland of your god

Still why do you argue over caste?

When you are wounded, is not it blood that gushes out?

When I, too, am wounded, is not it blood?

(Chandran 2006)

Pottan Teyyam employs the very weapon of advaita—non-duality, the oneness of being—against the proponent of that philosophical system. The philosopher realises his mistake and prostrates before the chandala who in turn blesses him. In Malayalam, the word 'pottan' is used for a fool but it may also refer to a deaf and mute person. For brahminical liturgy logic, reason and morality may appear foolish, but Pottan was no fool.

Like Ayyappa who admits all devotees without any distinction of caste, creed or class, teyyams do not respect the received brahminical wisdom on caste hierarchies. There are traces of Buddhism in the teyyam cult. The revolutionary tradition of teyyam is too obvious to be ignored. Ayyankali, Chattambi Swamy, Sree Narayana Guru and a host of others collectively took up the fight where Pottan Teyyam left it. The traditional mask dance of the dalits became a means to rebuke, ridicule and question the atrocities and injustices done to them. Teyyam dances and the group songs sung during the agricultural operations were a sort of inversions and defiance to the dominance of the high castes. During World War II, the Communist Party employed folk arts like teyyam, poorakkali and ottamtullal against black-marketeers and hoarders.

For the dalits, teyyam is a weapon in the struggle against the unjust social system that has marginalised them. Many teyyam stories contain criticism of untouchability and brahminism. The bulk of the two-hundred-odd teyyam artists in North Kerala are members or sympathisers of the Communist parties. The brahmins advise people to be pure and eat vegetarian food, while a teyyam god like Muthappa is all for eating meat, drinking and being jolly.

Of late there has been an intrusion of brahminical verses into the Dravidian tottam pattu—the ritual song sung during the teyyam—which is presumed to give it brahminic respectability. Palantayi Kannan, originally a tiyya martyr-deity, was Hinduised and turned into Vishnumurthy, the Vishnu avatar who devoured Hiranyakashipu. In the Hinduised version of the Sankara–Pottan face-off, the dalit disappears and in his place appears Lord Siva who blesses Sankara. The parayan victim of the caste system who advances solid arguments against caste is erased. T.V. Chandran writes: '[T]he subversive value of the Pottan's voice was put under the stronghold of the ideology of high-strata Hinduism through the interpolation of a story that appears in Sankara Digvijayam, a fourteenth century work which seeks to establish the supremacy of the great Indian philosopher Sri Sankaracharya' (Chandran 2006). According to this version, Sankara concludes that the person confronting him is no chandala but Lord Siva himself.

Donning the teyyam dress is the preserve of a host of oppressed caste devotees. The poor dalit who is teyyam today will be found slaving the next day in the landlord's paddy field for a pittance. During the teyyam season—from December to February—colourful teyyams teem northern Kerala to the accompaniment of loud drumbeat. As with the oracle of the Bhagavati temples in other parts of Kerala, the teyyams originated in what was once Kolathunadu—Kannur and

Kasargod districts of present-day Malabar.

Teyyam may have originated in the fertility cult associated with agriculture (Chandran 2006). Some scholars attribute its origin to the hero cults of the Sangam period. This ritual pageantry of North Kerala is a rare survivor of a pre-Aryan, non-brahminical religious system. It is said teyyams were tolerated as an acceptable safety valve to allow complaints against the misdeeds of the upper castes to be expressed in a ritualised and non-violent manner. During the colonial days Christian missionaries used to conduct house-to-house campaigns against teyyam and snake worship, calling them primitive and inhuman. This had a mixed response. The better-off tiyyas formed the Sree Jnanodaya Yogam to fight superstition and ended up conceding a brahminic halo to the local gods. Many oppressed communities in rural Kerala, however, had a visceral reverence for their gods and did not fall for the propaganda.

Mutthappa

Mutthappa, whose main shrine, called Madappura, is in Parassinikkadavu on the banks of the Valapattanam river in Kannur district, is the very face of emancipatory spirituality and a significant cultural entity in northern Kerala. He galvanised the poor tribals against the tyranny of the ruling Kuttiyot dynasty and gave them lessons in work and self-reliance. He rescued the slaves from the clutches of exploiters and other oppressors. Mutthappa stands in defiance of brahminical rules of holiness and pollution. Instead of idol worship there is a ritual enactment of Mutthappa every day at the Madappura. There is a simplicity and transparency about the mode of worship, unlike in upper caste temples where there is an obsession with 'purity' and where only brahmins are allowed into the sanctum, known often as the garba griha, the place of the womb—a dark, lightless place inaccessible to all but the priests. In contrast, wizened god Mutthappa heeds tearful cries for help and pleas from the have-nots and the bereaved and offers consolation and support. Those coming to worship at Parassinikkadavu are made to sit on the floor and fed rice and curry.

There are broad similarities between the myths relating to Ayyappa and Mutthappa. A baby was found in the forest by a childless brahmin couple. As he grew up, the boy grew weary of brahminic taboos and defied them without compunction—he would merrily go hunting, eat fish and meat, and drink liquor. He also began to climb palm trees and steal toddy. Chanthan, a toddy tapper, found that someone was stealing from his palm trees and on investigating found an old man perched up on a tree, sipping toddy. Chanthan aimed an arrow at the old man, calling him 'Mutthappa' (grandfather). An angry Mutthappa cursed Chanthan and turned him into stone. There are many such fantastical stories surrounding Mutthappa.

Among the uralans of the Madappura (which is what templels dedicated to Mutthappa are called) in Kasargod is a tiyya. Most priests come from the lower rungs of the caste hierarchy, while Mutthappa teyyams are enacted by dalits. Again, in Parassinikkadavu a dog is ever present by Mutthappa's side. The received brahminical wisdom about dogs being untouchable scavengers is challenged here. Perhaps the dog's presence is indicative of Mutthappa being a hunter god. It is also possible that his is an apparent case of ancestor worship—'mutthappa' means grandfather or granduncle—as in the Suyodhana shrine. Offerings to Mutthappa are mostly favourites of the common man—toddy, meat and fish. As in the case of Ayyappa, equality among the devotees is the norm in the Mutthappa cult. Like

Ayyappa, Mutthappa has never kept the untouchable at a distance. In fact, it was the other way about. In the past, caste Hindus would keep off the Madappura, which represented the ideology of lower caste revolt against brahmin culture and hegemony in Kerala. These days, savarna householders too come and pour out their woes before Mutthappa. There are Madappuras in Mumbai, Delhi and even in some of the Gulf countries.

Today concerted efforts are under way to Hinduise Mutthappa. In Delhi's Mayur Vihar, where the author of this book lives, the Sree Mutthappa Sewa Samithi, an organisation of devotees of the revered grand-uncle, claims in a booklet that Sree Muthappa is a Hindu deity worshipped commonly in Kannur district and adds rather apologetically that his worship does not follow the satvic (brahminical) form as in other Hindu temples. Inevitably perhaps, the cultural complexion of the shrine has undergone a transformation as Mutthappa is being gentrified and co-opted into the fold of Aryan deities. A foreword by a known pro-hindutva scholar, Priyadarshan Lal, to a book on the Mutthappa cult (*Sree Mutthappan—Aithihyavum Charitravum* by Latheesh Keezhallur) describes the deity as a confluence of Saivism and Vaishnavism. He claims that Mutthappa is a dalit incarnation of Lord Siva. The Madappura now displays the board 'kshetram' which word is normally used to describe a Hindu place of worship and relies on namboodiris for the performance of some rituals. Ganapati homams mark the beginning of the festival in November. The priest chants newly coined Sanskritistic mantras like "Sree Muthappaya Namah". As in temples banana and vegetarian delicacies like appam are offered to the deity. The worst part of the story is that members of the pulayan and other dalit communities are not allowed into the temple. Swami Anandathirthan, a radical social reformer who was a close disciple of the oppressed caste icon, Sree Narayana Guru, was roughed up when he tried to enter the Madappura in Parassinikkadavu along with a few lower caste children. The unending process of cultural destruction, attack on his fond disciple and the disbursal of toddy as prasadam perhaps prompted Narayana Guru to keep off the shrine when he came near Parassinikkadavu.

6

Buddha's Kin

AROUND 600 BCE, the Vedic religion with its yajnas and other wasteful and exploitative rituals faced a strong challenge from radical kshatriyas in eastern India. The birth of Buddhism and Jainism had its origin in the disillusionment of the kshatriyas with unproductive brahminism. The Buddhists rejected Vedic gods and campaigned against the yajnas in which countless cattle were butchered. There is the story about the Buddha barging into a yajna shed and herding out a band of sacrificial goats, earning the odium of the brahmin priests. Both Buddhism and Jainism were atheistic. The Buddha, who went all out against inequalities, giving hope to oppressed slaves, heralded the transformation of subcontinental production practices from slavery to serfdom.

Siddhartha Gautama attained nibbana (enlightenment), while meditating under the boughs of a fig tree. The place therefore came to be known as Bodh Gaya. The Mahabodhi Vihara in Bodh Gaya, some twenty kilometres from Patna, was built by Emperor Ashoka in the third century BCE and attracts pilgrims from various parts of India and abroad. Bodh Gaya is one of the four holiest places for Buddhists. Seventh century Chinese pilgrim Xuanzang described the place as 'the centre of the Buddhist world'. Gauda king Shashank, a Saivite contemporary of Harsha, emperor of the Vardhana dynasty, cut down the Bodhi tree and removed the Buddha image from the shrine near the tree and replaced it with a Siva Linga. In 1949, Vaishnavite and Saivite revivalists sought to Hinduise the shrine by getting the Bodh Gaya Temple Act passed.

Born in 599 BCE, Mahavira, the twenty-fourth thirthankara, sought to reform Jainism. Mahavira's emphasis was on devotion, prayer and charity instead of austere self-reliance and self-culture. Jainism teaches that for material progress to be profoundly solid, a spiritual culture has to develop. The Jain and Buddha legacies share the same ideological orientation; both rely on reason and critical analysis rather than on blind devotion. Scholars like Debiprasad Chattopadhyaya think that the rise of Buddhism and Jainism was a form of class struggle on the part of suppressed castes, while the fall of these non-theistic systems meant defeat of the lower suppressed castes by the upper castes using their political authority. B.R. Ambedkar also put forward his arguments along similar lines.

The rise and fall of Buddhist states and governments has great import in the historical democratic impulse in India. The democratic traditions continued till as late as the fourth century CE when Samudragupta wiped out the Buddhist republic states. Bimbisara, Ajatasatru, Kanishka I, Ashoka and the Greek king Menander were some of the rulers influenced by the values and principles preached by the Buddha. Many ancient Indian kings and authors of works on political thought theorised that the king owed his authority to the people. Continuing this tradition, the Buddha rejected brahminic theories of the state. For him, governance was to be based on mahasammat—full agreement between the ruler and the ruled. The Buddha who lived before

Socrates, and consequently before Plato and Aristotle, was much more than a philosopher—he was a political thinker with clear ideas on governance.

Gautama was a great shramana who belonged to the Sakya clan. He worked to formulate an alternative to the centralised and despotic monarchy of his time, championing the theory of 'bahujana sukhaya, bahujana hitaya' ('for the happiness of the majority, for the welfare of the majority'). His formula was that the state should provide capital to traders, ensure the necessary facilities to farmers, and fair and regular wages to workers. He maintained that crude punishment would not stamp out crime, the root cause of which lay in poverty, unemployment and socio-economic inequalities. The tradition of the election of the king continued till the twelfth century in some parts of India. Gautama's father was an elected ruler for some time. Maveli was perhaps an elected ruler, a representative of Kerala's glorious Buddhist heritage.

Ambedkar traced the origin of untouchability to the Buddhists' refusal to revere the brahmins and the latter's consequent hatred for the Buddhists. He equated the Buddhist raj with communism and believed that the Buddha could offer a lesson or two in revolution-making to the communists. The kind of communist society that Marx envisaged was the same as what Buddhism wanted to bring about. Unlike communism of the Russian type Buddhism brings about social change by a bloodless revolution, wrote Ambedkar. Contrast this with the social organisation envisaged by Kautilya which had the sanction of the Vedas. All he wanted was support and protection to the brahmins.

Democratic bhikhu sangha

The organisation of Buddhist monks—bhikku sangha—was a model of an ideal society, a classless organisation in which total harmony prevailed. The Buddha was very particular about equality in the bhikku sangha, drawing a parallel with rivers and the ocean: just as the Ganga and the Yamuna lose their identity when they reach the ocean, so he wanted his disciples, of all varnas and social categories, to forsake their home and go into homelessness, lose their own name and their old paternity and bear only one designation—shramana. In forming the sanghas, the Buddha is believed to have drawn inspiration from the way tribal gana sanghas of North India were organised, deriving their strength from the democratic and collective structure of their society. While classes did exist, the Buddha wanted the relationship between the worker and his master humanised. The prosperity of all people, not of a tiny minority, during the Buddhist era is vouchsafed by history. Yet, the Buddha was influenced by the patriarchal spirit of his time. Later Ananda persuaded him to shed his anti-woman prejudices, and allow women to join the sangha.

The bhikku sangha was a symbol of the people's aspirations and embodied democratic, communistic principles. In the sangha, the Buddha conducted experiments in democracy, freedom and equality. The Buddha who attacked the system of varnas appointed many individuals of so-called 'low birth' in key positions in the sangha. Unlike the brahmin priests, the monks led simple lives and mixed with the common people. There was no nepotism by design: Gautama's son Rahul remained an ordinary member of the sangha. There were rules of conduct for the monks and nuns codified in Vinaya Pitaka which is part of the Pali canon, Tipitaka (Three Baskets).

In spite of the communistic sanghas that the Buddha helped build, the forces operating in the larger class society remained unchanged. The Buddha approached the human condition in a scientific manner and advanced rational arguments to arrive at the truth. His missionaries who travelled to foreign lands never even dreamt of destroying the culture of any nation.

The Buddha was a free-thinker and democrat. 'Be you lamps unto yourselves,' was his advice. On his death bed he told his disciples not to believe anything merely because it is traditional, or because they themselves have imagined it. To not believe what the teacher tells them merely out of respect for him. Whatsoever, after due examination and analysis, is found to be conducive to the good, for the benefit, the welfare of all beings—believe and cling to that doctrine, and take it as your guide. The karma theory which he preached was unabashedly this-worldly, far different from what the Vedic religion trotted out.

Written in simple Pali, the language of the commoner, Buddhist works eschewed all esoteric claptrap. He provided no easy proscriptions and prescriptions. People were advised to work hard, shoulder to shoulder, for the prosperity of all. Man's liberation depended on his own actions, not on wasteful religious rituals. The Buddha argued that it is in a person's own interest to live virtuously. Like all other shramanas, the Buddha did not make a fetish of mental labour. Buddhism was a great religion if by that term we mean an earnest search for truth. It was not a religion in the conventional sense as the Buddha debunked the very idea of an almighty god. He hit at the very foundation of theism and conventional religious faith. The insistence on a social ethic without religious underpinnings distinguished early Buddhism from formal religions.

The Buddha's relentless campaign against ritualism earned

opprobrium from the elite. Small wonder that the faith mainly developed in areas like Magadha where the brahmins were weak. Following the schism in the faith and the triumph of the Mahayana creed, however, Buddhism had its radical teeth pulled out and it ceased to be a rational system. Mahayana Buddhists believe in gods and regard the Buddha as the greatest among them. There are elaborate ceremonies and rituals. Jawaharlal Nehru (1981) suggests that perhaps it was the brahmin Buddhists who were responsible for the Mahayana form developing along philosophical and metaphysical lines.

Under the patronage of Kanishka the Mahayana stream gained in popularity in India and abroad. In the Gupta period, Hindu kings patronised Buddhist institutions and built Buddhist shrines (Doniger 2009). Meanwhile, foreign invaders destroyed the great Buddhist centres of learning in eastern India and Kashmir. According to Doniger, Buddhism never recovered from the depredations of the Huns who killed monks and destroyed monasteries.

Since the puranas were an attempt to boost brahminic Hinduism, it is no wonder that the Mahabharata and the Vishnu Purana, among other works, listed the Buddha, whose influence spread even outside India, as one of the avatars of Vishnu. The revolutionary role that he played in Indian social life was completely ignored. The Jain and Buddhist legacies share the same ideological orientation. Both rely on reason and critical analysis rather than on blind devotion. It was obviously to attract his followers into the Hindu fold that he was included as one of the avatars. Neo-Buddhists rightly refuse to buy this avatar theory, arguing that the Buddha's was a revolt against the ritualism and inhuman inequalities of brahminical Hinduism. It was after the ideological threat from Buddhism died away that

Krishna's elder brother replaced the Buddha in the dasavatara. Buddhism exercised such a profound influence on Adi Sankara that some scholars call him a crypto-Buddhist.

Buddhism and Jainism in Kerala

In the Malayalam novel *Kochi*, Maveli wears a Buddhist aura. And the milieu is unapologetically Buddhist. In this re-reading of the Maveli story, K.L. Mohanavarma seeks to demythify and historicise the peasant king and his times. Maveli is depicted as the unfortunate victim of North Indian colonialism. The colonial rulers who marched into Kerala were the Guptas, who ruled over North India for well over a century and a half in the fourth and fifth centuries CE. Chandragupta was the founder of the dynasty and Kaachan his younger son. The Gupta period was the golden era of brahminism. Under the tutelage of Harisena, his brahmin guru who, being diminutive, earned the nickname Vamana, Kaachan boned up on the Vedas and other holy tomes. He mastered the intricacies of statecraft and became adept in the art of fighting. After he ascended the throne, he defeated the kings in northern and central India. He 'exterminated' the Naga kings and led his army to the South. He wanted to bring the rulers of the principalities in the South under his thumb, before moving on to the island of Lanka. After multiple battles, the boundary of the Gupta empire extends up to Tamizhakam. The Chola and Pandya regimes accepted the emperor's suzerainty. As though to proclaim to the world that he was the monarch of all he surveyed, including the oceans, Kaachan names himself Samudragupta, with the short-statured Harisena, as his trusted minister.

Going by Mohanavarma's fictional account, the Maveli–Harisena face-off took place on top of a hill in the heart of

Kochi where a Buddhist shrine had been constructed. It turns out to be a confrontation between right and wrong, between justice and injustice and, no less important, between Buddhism in which caste had no place and the chaturvarnya-based Vedic faith. Mahabali, who presided over a welfare state, enjoyed the wholehearted support of the regional satraps. The vihara on the hill doubled as a hospital-cum-research-centre where the sick and the ailing from various parts of the country flocked for treatment. At this medical centre Buddhist monks, who were legatees of Vagbhata, author of famous medical classics like Ashtangahrudayam, researched on and experimented with the rare herbs found in the green hills and plains of Kerala and found cures for various ailments. The presence of venomous reptiles in the region made the monks look for cures for snake poison.

Shrewd to the core, Samudragupta sends his shrewder brahmin envoy to the Kerala ruler's court. Harisena informs Maveli that the North Indian emperor wanted to build a Vishnu shrine in Kerala. Maveli volunteers to undertake the task himself, but the offer is politely turned down. What was sought was a small tract of land where Samudragupta can build a temple. The South Indian rulers had only heard about bloody wars, they had conquered minds with love, so Maveli did not suspect foul play. But soon he smells trouble and seeks support from the regional satraps in Kerala. But it is already too late—in a quick manoeuvre by bands of Guptan mercenaries, his allies are all disarmed and so are his own personal bodyguards. Maveli sends an envoy to Lanka seeking military help, but the king of the island, Meghavarna, has been taken under the custody of Samudragupta's men. The king of Lanka acquiesces to the North Indian ruler's overlordship.

Harisena robs the Buddhist monarch of his kingdom by a sleight of foot, as it were. The dwarfish brahmin raises his foot and claims what lay east and north. Another step and the rest of the country is snapped up. Where will he put his third step? Maveli bows before the cunning brahmin. Harisena put his foot on Maveli's head. The three steps formalise Samudragupta's domination over Mahabali. The helpless ruler realises that he has been cruelly cheated; he pays a heavy price for his generosity.

Maveli tells Harisena: 'You have defeated me but you can't throw me out of my people's hearts. I am leaving this land following in the footsteps of the great Buddha.' Samudragupta discovers that while he could defeat Bali and usurp his throne, the ideals for which the Buddhist monarch stood were invincible. The North Indian invader sheepishly concedes that his was a pyrrhic victory. On Thiruvonam day in Chingam every year the Buddhist ruler pays a visit to what was once his country. The regional rulers, ever loyal to Maveli, wait for that day to welcome the defeated emperor. The trikkakkarappans made of mud which Keralites place in their courtyards on Onam days are Buddhist tirthankaras. The powerful North Indian ruler was reluctant to meddle with the Buddhist culture of Mavelinadu.

There is a reference to Samudragupta in some other works which say that a Chera king resisted the North Indian emperor's invasion and that the celebration of this victory is what Onam originally indicated. Of course, history does not confirm such an invasion.

Against the backdrop of the spread of Buddhism that contributed immensely to Kerala's culture, it is possible that a Buddhist devotee did rule over Kerala in the distant past, that Mahabali was an ardent Buddhist who ruled at a time when the non-theistic faith reigned supreme in the spiritual and social life of the Malayali. Many scholars believe that the myth about the fall of Mahabali and the rise of Vamana represents the story of the snuffing out of Buddhism from Kerala where the rational shramanic faith flourished for well over a millennium. It is possible that the monastic order in which the Buddha experimented successfully with democracy provided the template for the description of the egalitarian Maveli kingdom. Many think Mahabali was the embodiment of shramana culture and that the brahmin boy signals the arrival of chaturvarnya. P. Palpu, the guiding spirit behind the Renaissance in Kerala, believed that Mahabali was a Buddhist who practised truth and justice in daily life and that Vamana was crafty brahminism in flesh and blood. It is quite likely that the land of milk and honey described in Onappattu is Kerala of the Buddhist era.

Like Palpu, scholars like Ajay Shekhar and P. Meerakkutty have placed Onam and the Maveli story in a Buddhist context and said that both the myth and the festival have strong Buddhist roots (Shekhar 2012). The gifting of clothes on the occasion of Onam is reminiscent of the Buddha presenting yellow clothes to new monks. There is also another story that Maveli's annual visit to Kerala was the brainchild of the Aryans who did not take kindly to the popularity of the Buddhist ruler, Pallivanapperumal, in the province. A conspiracy against the Perumal and the Buddhists may have been hatched at Trikkakkara, according to this theory. One of Kerala's leading poets, Ullur S. Parameswara Iyer, claimed that in the tenth century, Kerala leaders gathered at a mamankam (a huge fair held every twenty years) session and decided to invite the Cheraman Perumal, Bhaskara Ravi Varman, to rule over Kerala to patch up the differences among various village councils, to check Buddhism and breathe new life into the society. With this objective the new ruler launched a one-month-long festival in honour of Mahabali who was the darling icon of the people of Kerala.

There is reason to believe that Mahabali ruled his country keeping in mind the Buddhist theories of state and administration. Buddhism's gifts to Kerala included the politicisation of the concern for healthcare—the Onappattu contains a reference to the absence of illnesses and of infant mortality during Maveli's time. Buddhist monks set up hospitals and were adept medical researchers. Some Ashokan edicts mention medical services being rendered to both humans and animals. Kerala's particular form of Ayurvedic treatment which is now popular all over India is also a Buddhist legacy. So is vastu vidya, which deals with architecture and construction of houses. Vagbhatananda's famous work *Ashtangahridayam* mentions the 'rare physician' who is believed to be none other than the Buddha. Quite a few Pali words, 'palli', for example, have found their way into Malayalam. Some historians like M.G.S. Narayanan and Kesavan Veluthat rule out a Buddhist tradition in Kerala, but this is widely disputed.

Before small groups of Buddhists reached Kerala, the Jains had come looking for quiet surroundings and peace for meditation. There are traces of Jainism in Wayanad, Palakkad and Perumbavur. There was a Jain shrine in Paruvassery in Thrissur which later got converted into a Vishnu temple. The roots of the temples in Kallil near Perumbavoor and Chitral near Kuzhithura go deep into Jainism. Bharata of the Ramayana is claimed to be the presiding deity in the well-known Koodalmanikyan temple in Irinjalakkuda, but this was yet another case of gentrification. Many scholars identify the deity here with Jain monk Bharateswaran. The vegetarianism of upper caste Hindus is possibly a Jain legacy. Buddhism and Jainism brought a culture of literacy, education and the fine arts into this region. In places like Mathilakam and Kiliroor there were Buddhist and Jain universities and research centres in the early centuries of the first millennium that attracted intellectuals and students from all over the world. According to A. Sreedhara Menon, the two non-theistic religions retained their hold on the minds of the people till 800 CE.

'Though Buddhism and Jainism were fast declining owing to lack of royal patronage they still retained their hold on sections of the community,' says Sreedhara Menon. He attributes the rise of the bhakti movement to the decline of the heterodox religions. 'The Hindu reformers of the day became convinced that the continued hold of Buddhism and Jainism among common people stood in the way of the onward march of the Hindu religion in Kerala. In these circumstances the more inspired and scholarly among the Hindu devotees sought to exterminate their rival sects by evolving and popularising a new cult of bhakti, an intense surrender to a personal god in the form of Vishnu or Siva.'

The three-feet-tall Karumatikkuttan statue built in the eighth century in Ambalappuzha taluk in southern Kerala is believed to be the Buddha. The rice bowl of Kerala, Kuttanadu, probably got its name from 'Karumatikkuttan'. In the course of his visit to India in the 1960s, the Dalai Lama worshipped at the statue. A few hundred metres from the Buddhist shrine is a Krishna temple. The Buddha statues found in Mavelikkara, Bharanikkavu, Ambalappuzha, Pallippuram and elsewhere in South Kerala provide solid evidence of Kerala's Buddhist ancestry. The famous poet, Kodungallur Kunjukkuttan Thampuran, in talking about the later discovery of non-Hindu statues in Kerala suggests that it was Jainism which acquired greater popularity in the region. But one can assume that the populace did not distinguish between the two faiths. E.M.S. Namboodiripad claims that Kerala was the battlefield in which the struggle between the Vedic culture, on the one hand, and Buddhism and Jainism, on the other, became acute. He argues that many of the present-day Hindu temples had been Buddhist or Jain viharas at one time. A more or less similar story of struggles between Buddhism, Jainism, Saivism and Vaishnavism obtains in the neighbouring Tamizhakam.

The brahminical religion with its varna hierarchy was already in place in some parts of the region when the Buddhist ezhavas arrived. Buddhism displaced brahminism, pushed out the varna system and prevailed as the dominant creed for more than a millennium. In this ideological battle Namboodiripad sees the source of many aspects of Kerala history and culture. The former bureaucrat P.C. Alexander writes that the namboodiris used the weapon of 'social ostracism' to destroy Buddhist influence, besides turning viharas into temples.

Xuanzang's writings record that in the seventh century CE numerous Buddhist viharas in Malabar were destroyed or got converted into Hindu temples. The Buddha vihara at Trikkakkara became a Vishnu temple. After Kaveripoompattanam was taken by the sea, the Buddhists there migrated to Vanchi, which was the capital of the Cheras. So did monks from Kancheepuram which faced a famine. In the early years of the Christian era, Vanchi played host to a number of erudite scholars who engaged themselves in serious debates on religious and philosophical issues.

Festivals like Pooram, with the deity mounted on caparisoned elephants and accompanying panchavadyam and other musicals, being held in many Hindu temples, have their origin in Mahayana Buddhism. Remember, tuskers had a prominent place in the Buddhist cultural scheme. Buddhism and Buddhist values of love, compassion, social justice and a rational approach to life inspired the creative energies of a large number of Malayalam writers.

Buddhist monks set up many viharas which provided free education to people belonging to every caste and religion. There was a great centre of learning in Vanchi which provided facilities for higher studies in atheistic disciplines like Lokayata, Sankhya and Aajeevika. Pained at inequalities and the denial of learning to those at the bottom of the social pyramid, the Buddha set up a small educational institution in Nalanda. Long before Oxford and Cambridge, it blossomed into a great seat of learning, with hostels for students and teachers. It was in Nalanda that the Vajrayana form of Buddhism sprouted. The Vajrayana faith assumed its full glory in Vikramashila University and in the thirteenth century travelled to Tibet and Mongolia. The Buddhists thus laid in Kerala the foundation of a sound system of education, on which Christian missionaries built later. According to P. Palpu, Buddhism in Kerala was not confined to a particular community; it was the reigning religion of the entire region. Up until the sixth century CE, the majority in the region were Buddhists. This social order was destroyed after the brahmins appropriated power. The bulk of the Buddhists got absorbed into Hinduism at the bottom of the hierarchical scale. However, exception was made in the case of some scholars who were useful for the new social order. For example, those who were experts in medicine were given the sacred thread and brahminised; they are today's illustrious Ayurvedic physicians. Those who worked in viharas were sucked into the brahmin theocracy.

Palpu opines that the killing of kshatriyas recounted in the Parashurama myth was a displaced sign of the violent killing of Buddhists on the Kerala coast. He believed that Bhargavarama killed the Buddhist rulers of India twenty-one times round. 'Parashurama', said Palpu in a letter to Mahatma Gandhi, 'also usurped this ancient country on account of its prosperity and divided it among a few brahmins whom he had manufactured here or imported from elsewhere, and was therefore deified as the miraculous spiritual 'Creator' of this country and donor of it to the few brahmins in expiation of his enormous sins, as if usurpation and gift of other's lands and property would atone for any murders at all' (Sanu 2013).

Buddhism flourished in Kerala for well over a millennium, from 300 BCE to 800 CE. The age of the Kulashekharas, the last of the Cheras, saw the decline of Buddhism and what is described as the subsequent revival of Hinduism. But the fact of the matter is that Hinduism never did enjoy any position of primacy to be 'revived'. It was a minor religion, one among the many that were practised in the region. What happened during the Kulshekhara rule then was a violent stamping out of rival religions and the establishment of an autocracy of the Hindu value system.

By 600 BCE, South India left its days of barbarism far behind and advanced to modernity. People in Kerala and elsewhere in South India had taken to food-grain cultivation on a large scale. The credit for this should go to the shramanas—Buddhists and Jains—who upheld the importance of toiling hard and an ethical life. It was during the Buddhist age that new farming and irrigation methods, including the use of the ploughshare and draught animals, were developed in Kerala. The monks themselves worked in the fields and became role models for the common people. Jainism too put farmers on a high pedestal. Agriculture became predominant followed by breeding of cattle. All this resulted in the promotion of people-friendly productive forces and consequently there was widespread prosperity. The new faith discouraged wanton killing of animals and placed stress on the cultivation of pulses and grain. Various underprivileged sections in Kerala trace their roots to Buddhism. Even some Christians maintain that they were Buddhists before they converted. Palpu also theorised that the various rites and practices that became part of the Christian tradition in the West had its origin in Indian Buddhism. The common elements included monasteries, nunneries, tonsured monks, observance of celibacy, rosary beads and confession. Even the teachings of Christ bear a striking similarity to the gospel of the Buddha. In his presidential address at the SNDP Yogam in 1936, Palpu argued that 'by rendering universal love and service without any distinction of caste, creed, race or language, and by their general character and conduct, our forefathers here had, long before the birth of Christ, made themselves 'true Christians'.

Any account of Buddhism in Kerala will not be complete unless you mention the ezhava community. The ezhavas, who constitute an intermediate caste, were originally migrants from Ceylon. Mahayana Buddhism, it is claimed, came to Kerala in a roundabout manner from Lanka after Emperor Ashoka's time, in the early centuries of the common era. The caste appellation 'ezhava' was probably a derivative from 'Eelam', Tamil for Lanka. 'Tiyyan', another name for the community, especially in North Kerala, was claimed to be a modification of 'dwipan' (islander). They are known as chovans—the etymological root of this name, according to C.V. Kunjuraman, comes from the

Tamil word 'choaka' which meant a mendicant or a Buddhist monk. Kunjuraman, however, also believed that the ezhavas were an indigenous Buddhist community.

The Buddhist influence on Narayana Guru, the great social revolutionary and sage, is also consequential. Some of his close disciples like Sahodaran Ayyappan described the thinker-savant as 'Kerala's Buddha'. Narayana Guru was a keen student of Buddhist and Jain philosophy (Chandramohan 2016). In the early twentieth century Buddhism influenced the radical namboodiris who fought to bring about reforms in their community, under the guidance of the Guru. Sharada Madham, which Narayana Guru consecrated in 1911, resembles a Buddha vihara. The erection of this temple dedicated to Sharada, the goddess of learning, was a new chapter in Narayana Guru's religious understanding. He rejected caste distinctions as irrational and practised what he preached. The uplift of the pulayans and the parayans was a crucial part of his life's mission. In building up his ashram, Narayana Guru followed in the footsteps of the Buddha, who had no hesitation in admitting devotees of the oppressed castes in his sanyasi sangha. Similarly, Narayana Guru, himself of the ezhava caste, had students from all across the caste spectrum. In his ashram, all the students lived, dined, prayed and studied together. They used the same bathing facilities and they cooked their food collectively. When guests came visiting, they were served by pulayan students. As P. Chandramohan notes, 'Whenever prominent caste-conscious people came to the ashram, the Pulayans would serve food to them, and on many occasions, the guru made it a point to introduce these servers of food to the visitors as Pulayans. When quarrels broke out between caste Hindus and non-caste Hindus, he was always on the side of the latter' (2006). Sree

Narayana Guru followed in the footsteps of the Buddha when he defied the rules of casteism formulated by Vedic brahminism and created a new social sphere where no caste distinctions were observed. In fact, he insisted that his teaching centres be primarily for the benefit of avarna students.

Ezhava stalwarts like Padmanabhan Palpu were proud of Kerala's Buddhist past. In the 1920s, Buddhism had become an important concern for many of them. Leaders like C.V. Kunjuraman, C. Krishnan, E.V. Ayyakkutti and Sahodaran Ayyappan argued that, historically, ezhavas were not practitioners of the Hindu religion and that conversion to Buddhism may offer them an egalitarian alternative, much like B.R. Ambedkar's declaration in 1956. Krishnan, the editor of *Mitavadi*, became an active campaigner for Buddhism after 1922, organising events in Calicut, many of them with the participation of monks from Lanka. At a function held on Vaisakha Paurnami in Ernakulam in 1926, Krishnan and Ayyappan declared their allegiance to Buddhism. Ayyappan believed that the ezhavas were once Buddhists who had established a utopian society based on equality and fraternity in Kerala. Kunjuraman wrote several articles on Buddhism in Kerala in journals like *Kaumudi* and *Mitavadi* in the 1920s and, in the context of lower caste agitations demanding temple entry, mooted mass conversion of ezhavas to Buddhism, causing demographic anxiety among caste Hindus. This suggestion led to disagreements and debates among the ezhavas and in the SNDP Yogam.

Although Sree Narayana Guru was influenced by the Buddha's teachings he did not explicitly support or oppose moves towards conversion. The guru rejected the non-egalitarian values of brahminism, but did not completely break from the

Hindu tradition. He was more interested in the humanistic concepts in the Vedic culture. He was also impressed by Sankara's advaita. Guru was a practical vedantin who spoke in a language intelligible to the common man.

Although they were anti-Hindu in the beginning, the Buddhist ezhavas too ultimately joined the ranks of the Hindus and got pushed to the lower rungs of the caste ladder. The ezhavas continued to resist the new domination, which resulted in their stigmatisation. The ezhava way of life which placed stress on rationalism, equality and virtue rather than on blind faith and empty rituals got crushed under the weight of Aryanisation. It did not take long for the ezhavas to forsake their rationalist Buddhist heritage. The ezhavas who suffered caste discrimination at the hands of the upper castes perpetrated the same crime on those castes which were considered lower than them in the caste hierarchy.

Treated as untouchables by the upper castes, the ezhavas considered themselves above the dalit castes. Sahodaran Ayyappan was dubbed parayan Ayyappan and his friends were denounced as parayan choans. The ezhava elite who formed the Sree Narayana Dharma Paripalana Sangham (SNDP) treated the pulayans and the parayans as untouchables and kept them off their temples. Several ezhava temples closed their doors to dalits. When Ayyappan organised inter-dining with the lower caste parayans, the ezhavas in Cherai found themselves divided. The powerful organisation of orthodox ezhavas, 'Vijnana Vardhini Sabha', stood opposed to Ayyappan and his followers. He was doused with red ants and cow dung at their instigation Chandramohan (2006) mentions an incident in North Kerala where a pulayan and his sister were beaten up for not stepping aside to allow some ezhavas to pass unpolluted. In 1924 some orthodox ezhavas even moved the court in Paravur against Narayana Guru over the entry of dalits into the Kalikavu temple.

Thunchath Ezhuthachan

Thunchath Ezhuthachan, the father of Malayalam language who broke the brahmin monopoly over knowledge, was a product of Kerala's rich Buddhist–Jaina tradition. In the thirteenth and fourteenth centuries, farmers, traders and workers began to unite against brahmin domination. Ezhuthachan, who lived at the end of this era, brazened out the namboodiris and their henchmen, the nairs. The Buddhist tradition had all but vanished from Kerala but the bhakti-era of the sixteenth and seventeenth centuries saw the rebirth of the profound humanistic values of the heterodox faith. With this difference that bhakti poetry was emotional unlike Jainism and Buddhism both of which appealed to reason. The bhakti movement cut across caste and religious barriers and sought to democratise and humanise Hinduism. The devotion was not temple-centred. Neither in the Saivite nor in the Vaishnavite stream of bhakti was there any place for a priest to mediate between the worshipper and the worshipped. Kerala's bhakti poets included two namboodiris, Poonthanam, who pooh-poohed the hollow pretensions of brahmins and their obsession with yajnas, and Cherusseri.

The ancestors of Ezhuthachan, the most outstanding poet of Kerala's bhakti movement, had migrated to Malabar from the other side of the Western Ghats. A senior member of the Zamorin's palace in Kozhikode suggested to them to teach the illiterate shudras and gave them the title 'Ezhuthachan', literally 'father of letters'. Under brahmin dispensation the shudras were not allowed the luxury of education. Heeding the royal order, members of the community assumed the garb of society's pedagogues, setting up elementary schools in southern Malabar. The Buddhists who were later forced to convert to Saivism or Vaishnavism played an important role in fostering literacy and education among the common people. There was considerable female presence in the system of ezhuthupallis or kudippallikkoodams (residential schools) run by aasans and aashattis (male and female teachers). Children who were brought to kudippallikkoodams to learn the letters would do sundry chores for the guru. That system anticipated the primary school system of the modern era, minus the extraction of free labour of course.

On Vijayadashami day every year Thunchan Parambu (Thunchan's turf) teems with hundreds of wide-eyed children who come for their initiation into the world of letters. Time was when the aasans would make the little ones scribble, in rice or sand, 'Nanam Monam' or 'Namothu Chinatham', a Pali rendering of the Sanskrit phrase 'Namostu Jina te' which means, 'I bow before Jinadeva [the Buddha]'. Gradually, the initiation ceremony got Hinduised, the old invocation giving way to the unmistakably brahminical 'Hari Sree Ganapathaye Nama'. Functions are held across Kerala and in the diaspora, marking Vijayadashami the culmination of the Navarathri festival. Vidyarambham, translatable as initiation into knowledge, is arranged at home and at public functions by religious and educational institutions and cultural organisations, with the parent or some prominent cultural figure, often a famous litterateur, acting as the guru. The ceremony is also held in churches where the priests make toddlers—not necessarily Christian—write their first letters. Ezhuthachan was the first mass-educator in Kerala; he introduced Ramayana and Mahabharata to the oppressed castes. He was born in July or August 1496 and suffered ill-treatment at the hands of the namboodiris who were envious of the poet's talent and erudition. Touring the country acquainting himself with its folk culture, Ezhuthachan learnt the kilippattu metre from the unlettered folks. Life outside Kerala brought him into touch with the Ramayana and Mahabharata stories. There is a view that it was on the suggestion of the ruler of Chempakasseri, who handed him a copy of the Telugu Ramayana, that Ezhuthachan translated the epic into Malayalam. He also relied on tenth century poet Somadeva's *Adhyatmaramayana*.

Till Ezhuthachan's day the epics were available only in Sanskrit—a language the lower castes were not permitted to learn. He translated the Ramayana and the Mahabharata into simple Malayalam, though not word by word. He worked to raise Malayalam, a victim of brahminic contempt, to the level of what was regarded as the language of the gods. Ezhuthachan employed the Dravidian language to empower the common man, to retrieve the self-respect of a colonised people. He worked to free the language from the shackles of Sanskrit and Tamil, virtually shaping a new language. Similarly, in Maharashtra bhakti poets like Tukaram and Ekanath earned brahmin odium because they wrote in their mother tongue, which the upper castes considered impure. Ezhuthachan's translations of the Ramayana and the Mahabharata became immensely popular among the non-brahmin castes and spurred a cultural revolution of sorts. In the Malayalam *Adhyatma Ramayanam,* Ezhuthachan adopted the poetic method of making a parrot narrate the story. During the translation he often addresses a certain 'Sharika paithal', may be his daughter's pet name. Apparently, in his work he took considerable assistance from his daughter.

Ezhuthachan revolted against intolerance and superstitions.

He learnt the Vedas and the Upanishads although he was not a brahmin. He believed that whatever his or her religion, caste or economic status, everyone should be given education. He apologises mockingly to the brahmins for his 'sin' of writing the *Adhyatma Ramayana*. Some scholars opine that his much-criticised addiction to liquor and craze for meats reflected his own way of rejecting the tyranny of brahminism.

Again, Ezhuthachan's works like the *Mahabharatam* are not word-by-word translations. The longish Bhagavad Gita is dismissed in a few lines. After all, several modern scholars have argued that the Gita provided the ideological scaffolding for the caste system. Krishna tells Arjuna that he created the four-fold varna system (IV.13), and that the shudras, vaisyas and women have come from the womb of sin (papayoni, IX.32). D.D. Kosambi says the Gita, which was an interpolation, was written in the days of Gupta king Baladitya in the sixth century CE, and was aimed at checking the popularity of Buddhism. Perhaps there was a Buddhist hiding in the doubting Arjuna, hence Krishna's longish peroration. The bhakti poets have by and large chosen to ignore the Gita, while dalit writers have understandably been critical of the work.

Ezhuthachan wanted to send out a healthy message of social harmony and equality to the people. Through devotional works he sought to teach and make available a variety of cultural resources to the shudras. He refused to accept the undemocratic brahmin culture but he too, like Narayana Guru, refused to completely break away from the Hindu tradition. Nor did he reject Aryan themes wholesale; perhaps he had his social limitations.

Even so, there are enough indications of Ezhuthachan's anti-caste orientation. In *Adhyatma Ramayanam*, Rama reminds his younger brother Lakshmana that caste pride is meaningless. In the forest, Rama tells the adivasi woman, Sabari, that when it comes to bhakti, caste and gender differences have no meaning. Every living being is part of paramatma, Hanuman is told. Ezhuthachan wielded the ezhuthani (iron stencil) first to pierce the inhuman varna system and later to translate the epics, as Malayalam poet Edasseri Govindan Nair has put it. Of course, in Ezhuthachan's Ramayana, we see Rama slaying Baali, brother of Sugreeva, and Ravana, the rakshasa monarch of Lanka, but the funerals accorded to them are as solemn as the one given to king Dasaratha in Ayodhya.

Conclusion

FOR DECADES, women of menstruating age were disallowed from entering the Sabarimala complex, a temple which is said to symbolise Kerala itself. The reason given is that Ayyappa, the main deity, is a naishtik brahmachari. This restriction was contested on the grounds that it violated the fundamental rights of women. The case dragged on for twelve long years. The court heard twenty-four people including representatives of the Pantalam family, who have a stake in the temple, and the tantri or chief priest. It deputed two legal luminaries as amicus curiae and heard their views. The exclusion of women of menstruating age in the temple, a Constitution Bench of the Supreme Court ruled by a 4–1 majority on 28 September 2018, is unconstitutional, nothing short of unconstitutional untouchability. While the then Chief Justice of India, Justice Dipak Misra, and Justices R.F. Nariman, A.M. Khanvilkar and D.Y. Chandrachud ruled against the ban on women in the 10–50 age group, the sole dissenting judge, Justice Indu Malhotra, felt the restriction was in pursuance of an essential religious practice.

The ban on women's entry is by all accounts a recent development in Sabarimala, although some brag that it is 'centuries-old'. The Travancore Devaswam Board (TDB) which manages the temple had admitted in the Kerala High Court that till 1950 women of all ages went to the temple to christen their children or serve the infants their first token meal in Lord Ayyappa's presence. This was evidenced by receipts for payments made by the TDB. And, the 'rule' has been flouted umpteen times with impunity: there are reports of members of the Pantalam 'royal' family, which has a stake in the temple affairs, having flouted. Also reported was the fact that the TDB allowed the shooting of a dance number for a film, on the Sabarimala steps after accepting the necessary fees (Kumar 2018). In any case, the historic judgement threw the gates of Sabarimala open to women of all ages, ushering in a new age of inclusivity and returning the holy mountain to its egalitarian roots. But what followed was a shameful display of sexism and conservatism which brought the essential patriarchal nature of Malayali society to the fore.

Obscurantism and patriarchal and communal prejudices bubbled over in all its fearsome ugliness when an unprecedented hyper-mobilisation of the so-called believers began in Sabarimala. State BJP chief P.S. Sreedharan Pillai claimed later that he had used the 'golden opportunity' to implement his party's agenda and that other protesters had walked into his trap. Upper caste groups—brahmins and nairs—and the state unit of the Congress served as tools of the Sangh parivar. The Hindu Right stage-managed the violent show in the crudest manner possible. At a meeting in Kollam, in the august presence of a gleeful Sreedharan Pillai, a mediocre film actor, Kollam Thulasi who belongs to his party screamed at the 'idiots of the Supreme Court'. Worse, he made the chilling suggestion that women who dared go to Sabarimala should be torn into two, and one piece should be sent to Delhi (where the Supreme Court is located) and the other thrown at the feet of the CPI (M) chief minister, Pinarayi Vijayan. Vijayan, on the other hand, maintained, as he should, that the Supreme Court verdict would be implemented.

So, after the temple opened its doors for the month's puja, hooligans rudely checked the date of birth of women pilgrims and prevented those who were between 10 and 50 years from moving towards the shrine, much like the anti-beef vigilantes of the North. Protestors mouthed abuses and forced pilgrims to get down from vehicles on the way to the hill shrine. Women correspondents and camerapersons of media outlets like the *New York Times*, CNN and NDTV were booed and heckled. Windows of their vehicles were broken. Junior priests joined the protest sit-in. The tantri threatened a lock-up of the temple in case women 'defiled' the place and gushed that a movement of the Hindus was making fast progress. Sreedharan Pillai revealed later that the tantri had consulted him on the lock-up threat. In the subsequent days, of course, the police rounded up quite a few people guilty of harassing pilgrims. Ironically, the educated women of Kerala who were in the forefront of the loud campaign, led by the BJP's women's wing, to save Sabarimala from their own allegedly impure presence had not raised their voice against the rise in prices or the increasing violence against their sisters. Some see an 'anti-Renaissance' wave in Kerala, like the counter-Reformation in Europe unleashed by the Catholic Church after the Martin Luther-led Reformation. In the midst of such tumult, two brave women, Bindu Ammini and Kanaka Durga, got into the Sabarimala complex through the staff entrance. It was a historic moment. Before this, several women, including the activist Rehana Fathima had unsuccessfully attempted the same feat—Fathima even cited the Advaita theory of the oneness of being, thereby repeating Pottan Theyyam's gesture, to justify her actions. In these acts a clear message was sent out, no amount of oppression and obscurantist legislation could withstand the might of justice and the demand for equality.

As news of this spread, right-wing groups went into a tizzy, pelting police vehicles with stones and wreaking havoc. In this violence, one struggles to see any semblance of a religion. What was the point of all this frenzy, of this unnecessary and ignorant anger? Were they holding on to 'Hinduism'? Throughout this book I have tried to problematise this notion, that Kerala has some kind of an essential 'Hindu' identity. Will you count as Hindus the devotees of Ravana, mortal enemy of Rama for whom hindutva forces are planning a temple in Ayodhya? But what does 'religion' itself mean then? A popular definition of religion, is that it is a unified system of beliefs and practices relative to sacred things. Myths, memory and tradition shape the modern sub-national identity of any land. The religious tradition obtaining in Kerala is more democratic and less savarna than the combative sanatan Hinduism that perpetually seems to be marching onwards to Ayodhya.

As E.M.S. Namboodiripad puts it in a much-debated Malayalam work, 'Neither the axe of Parasurama nor the advaita of Sankara, or even 2,000 years of continuous Brahmin power, have been able to destroy the non-Brahmin way of life' (Menon 2011). A mythical asura ruler who was the enemy of the Hindu gods is the darling of the people in Kerala and stays at the epicentre of their most important festival; they worship non-Aryan deities like Ayyappa and Mutthappa, anti-heroes like Suyodhana, who is the villain of the Mahabharata, and goddesses who have arisen from the people's reverence for nature. There are sizeable Christian and Muslim population in this state and it has a deep-rooted legacy of Jainism and Buddhism. Militant subaltern protest and resistance movements against the tyranny of the upper castes led to the rise of the Left and shaped the identity of Kerala, and made it stand out as an example all across the world.

It is against this socio–political backdrop that the efforts of the Hindu communal Sangh parivar to find a toehold in the state should be seen. The Bharatiya Jan Sangh never won a seat in the state legislature, let alone in the Lok Sabha from Kerala. Its successor, the Bharatiya Janata Party, was unrepresented in the House till 2016; in the election that year, almost seven decades after independence, the party won a solitary seat in the Assembly. However, the poor electoral performance of the BJP should not make anyone underestimate the deep hindutva undercurrent sweeping the state. There are more Rashtriya Swayamsewak Sangh shakhas in Kerala than in most other provinces. Through its many feeder organisations, publications and its television channel, exploiting the fears about Christians and Muslims emerging as powerful religious groups, the Sangh parivar has been spreading the communal venom among the gullible.

It must be remembered that there are no principles the Sangh parivar is trying to uphold in its bullish dash to amass as much power as it can. Take the Sabarimala issue. Even here, the sanghis haven't had a consistent stand. The petition against the ban on women of menstruating age had been filed in the Supreme Court in 2006 by a few women who were close to the Sangh parivar. P. Parameswaran, hindutva ideologue and supremo of the Thiruvananthapuram-based 'think'-tank Bharatiya Vichar Kendra, had said as early as 2006 that he favoured the entry of women of every age for praying in Sabarimala. Senior BJP leaders have said that their party shared this stand. In the days following the Supreme Court verdict, the Sangh parivar mouthpiece *Janmabhumi* editorially welcomed the judgment and carried articles supporting women's entry.

What then prompted the Hindu Right's flip-flop? There is more to the cacophonous protests than fascination for time-honoured temple customs and practices. It was a political move. Not only did demonetisation, Prime Minister Narendra Modi's brainchild, not touch the tip of the huge black money iceberg, it smashed the unorganised sector and caused massive loss of jobs, besides resulting in over a hundred deaths and huge hardships to the people. The government was found badly wanting in handling the falling rupee, the rising oil prices and, much more importantly, the agrarian distress. No solution was in sight for the NPA crisis that has crippled the banking sector. As for the dubious Rafale fighter jet deal with France and the undue favours allegedly given to the Anil Ambani group, such frequent and new revelations added to the Sangh parivar's embarrassment. Nor is the Kerala BJP which, for the first time in Indian history, sent a lone candidate to the assembly in the last election, free of corruption and in-fighting. There was the medical college scandal which came to light because of factional feuds. Not long ago a few members of the party, which arrogates to itself a monopoly of patriotism, were arrested on a charge of printing fake currency notes. All this sullied the image of the BJP, including that of its Kerala unit. Essentially, the power-hungry party stands for no principles, but all the same, being right-wing, needs to constantly appear to be the protector of national and traditional interests.

With the Lok Sabha elections around the corner, a worried Sangh parivar badly needed an issue that would take people's attention off the rampant corruption and pressing problems like unemployment and price rise. The sectarian BJP jumped at the Supreme Court judgment—what better issue than one related to religion, rather a pseudo-religion? The Sangh parivar deftly injected religiosity into the protests. The protesters did not shout secular slogans. They chanted 'Ayyappa, Ayyappa' and carried 'Save Sabarimala' placards. In the past the faithful went to Sabarimala to seek protection from Ayyappa; now, ironically, they were offering protection to the god!

In the last few decades the very character of the Sabarimala pilgrimage has changed. In the past, as many as 41 days used to elapse between the wearing of the string of beads and 'kettunara' (filling of what is known as 'irumutikkettu' or 'pallikkettu' as a prelude to leaving home for the hill temple bare foot). During this period devotees led a life of austerity and strict discipline. Getting up early in the morning, they took a dip in the cold water of a river or a pond, fighting the chill with chants of 'Swamy Sharanam,' and 'Ayyappa Sharanam'. Today the bulk of the devotees finish the pilgrimage in a couple of days; irumutikkettu is available at the Pampa for a few hundred rupees. The colour of the devotee's cloth used to be black; now saffron is also in the mix.

Ayyappa has been a silent spectator to the selective adaptation and removal of traditional customs. The 'believers' looked the other way when the shudras and adivasis were pushed to the margins of religious life in Sabarimala. Only now, in the wake of the recent Supreme Court verdict, has it dawned on some people in Kerala and in the diaspora, including in Delhi, that traditional customs are being increasingly meddled with, that the caste wars of yore never really ended. The only self-righteous concern of the self-styled believers who conducted prayer marches in Kerala and elsewhere and formed an Achara Samrakshana Samity' (Organisation to Protect custom) is this custom—of the temple not admitting women of the 10–50 age group. Apparently, the 'believers' do not include the subaltern sections whose rights are taken away under the watchful eyes of the TDB.

Incidentally, as the government of Kerala told the High Court in an affidavit, Sabarimala is more a tribal or Buddhist shrine than Hindu. Yet, this is not the first time the hill temple provided a 'golden opportunity', to borrow Sreedharan Pillai's phrase, to fanatics for Hindu mobilisation. In June 1950 the temple saw a big fire which wrought massive destruction. The idol was partly destroyed. It was portrayed as the result of a well-laid-out plot. An organisation, Hindu Mahamandal, called a hartal in Thiruvananthapuram. In 1983 a granite cross was found at Nilakkal, 20 km away from the Sabarimala temple. Someone spread a rumour of a church being built at the spot where the cross was found. As saffron-clad swamys marched to the site of the proposed church, the police clashed with the protesters. The potential crisis was defused thanks to the presence of a few mediators and sober individuals in both Hindu and Christian camps. The church authorities made it clear that they had no intention to build a Christian place of worship at the cost of religious harmony.

Hindutva in Kerala

The Kerala Renaissance of the first half of the mid-twentieth century was a secular phenomenon, in which the hindutva elements did not have any role. In 1942, however, three Maharashtrian pracharaks came to the province and started work from three important cities—Thiruvananthapuram, Kochi and Kozhikode. Five years later emerged the first batch of Malayali pracharaks who worked among students, workers and adivasis. Today the Sangh parivar controls feeder organisations like Balagokulam, a Malayalam daily newspaper,

Janmabhumi, weekly *Kesari* and even the Janam TV channel, and has its sympathisers in various institutions and the media. The students' organisation ABVP (Akhil Bharatiya Vidyarthi Parishad) has been active in schools, colleges and universities. The usual fascistic tactic of spreading a rumour about Hindus becoming a minority in Kerala in the not-too-distant future, is under way. Hindutva ideologues have sought to prove that the Christian and Muslim populations are swelling in Kerala, while that of Hindus has come down. The sinister implications of such comments should be clear to anyone who is aware that the Sangh parivar equates Indian identity with Hindu. What is conveniently forgotten is the fact that what obtains in Kerala is, as we have argued, a multiplicity of religions which are opposed to a monolithic Hindu mould.

The Sangh parivar has been far from comfortable with the conjectural cultural mosaic character of various 'minor' religions in India. The state saw several attempts to dismantle the subaltern regime of worship—with some success. Over the decades the hindutva forces have injected various facets of north Indian religious life into the socio-political life of Kerala—Raksha bandhan, Rama devotion, Ganesha festival, shobha yatras, et al. Raksha bandhan is the North Indian brahminical ritual of sisters tying 'rakhis' on their brothers' wrists. Amusingly, many of those who display rakhi on their wrists do not know who should tie the rakhi on whose wrists and when. Notices pasted on walls in villages summon cadres to a particular place where an activist of the RSS or Vishwa Hindu Parishad, not a loving sister, waits with the rakhis. Sections of educated people have been playing sucker to the exotic rakhi culture, displaying the rakhi on wrists for days together. Tarun Vijay of the RSS got women MPs belonging to the BJP to send rakhis to the brother of an RSS victim of the mindless murder politics of northern Kerala.

The Kshetra Samrakshana Samitis (temple protection committees) have played a key role in the Hinduisation of pre-Aryan places of worship, and renovation of old temples as part of their efforts to spawn hyper-religiosity and foster a temple-based way of life. They conduct Bhagavad Gita classes; as if to atone for the sin of ignoring Rama in spiritual life, the hindutva lobby has sponsored a 'Ramayana month'. The idea was mooted by Parameswaran at a 'Vishala Hindu Sammelanam' in Ernakulam in 1982. The conference was a landmark event as the leaders of various caste organisations who participated in the meeting pledged to work for Hindu consolidation. Since then, the Ramayana is being read in the Malayalam month of Karkitakam (July–August) in middle and upper caste homes and places of worship in a milieu of profound devotion. Of late, with the blessings of the Sangh parivar, the powerful transport lobby has been organising a ritual 'four-temple trip', the temples being those where Rama and his three brothers are purported to be the chief deities. It was a case of business and religion coming together in sinister synergy.

The Sangh parivar has been trying to turn every innocuous issue into a controversy. Claiming a monopoly of the Ramayana tradition, in 2015 the Sangh parivar it forced M.M. Basheer, a writer who happened to be a Muslim to drop his column on the epic in a newspaper. A sentence or two that rolled off the tongue of a character in the Malayalam novel *Meesha*, which was being serialised in the respectable *Mathrubhumi Weekly*, were seen as anti-brahmin and anti-woman. The serialisation was discontinued following noisy protests from a section of the readers.

The Hindu Right has worked out a catch-them-young strategy that produces potential raw material for its student and youth activism. Janmashtami, Krishna's birthday, is celebrated by the Sangh parivar affiliate, Balagokulam, in the most un-Malayali way—with tiny tots marching in what are called shobha yatras. The celebrations often turn bizarre and inhumane: on Ashtami Rohini day in 2017, in Payyannur in northern Kerala, a three-year-old child was dressed up as infant Krishna and tied to an artificial peepal leaf mounted on a vehicle and kept there for several hours till police intervention ended the infant's ordeal. Kerala has also been seeing the dumping, preceded by pujas, of Ganesha idols in rivers and the sea. There is stiff opposition from many cultural and political organisations to the introduction of alien rituals and festivals in this southern state.

Malayali pracharaks of hindutva organisations are perhaps unaware that in seeking to impose an alien religious culture on the people of Kerala, it disrespects indigenous culture and ethos. Parivar affiliates in the North do not, as a return gesture, celebrate Kerala festivals like Onam and Vishu. The Sangh parivar's respect for South Indian culture is but skin-deep. During a recent television channel debate Tarun Vijay suggested condescendingly that North Indians were forced to 'live with' the 'black' people of the South. As if the dark-complexioned South Indians are on sufferance in this country! He forgot that Krishna, a pre-Aryan tribal deity to begin with, who grew into the much-worshipped avatar of Vishnu, was not fair-complexioned. There was hue and cry in Parliament and outside over Vijay's comment following which he issued a retraction. But he had, if unwittingly, let out the diabolic hindutva fundamentalist prejudice. Of late, ignoring angry protests, the BJP-led central government has launched a campaign to promote Hindi at the expense of regional languages. Place names in English on the milestones on national highways were re-lettered in Hindi and Devanagari numerals began to appear on currency notes. But this should not fool any one, all of this is just a smoke-screen to distract or dissuade us from looking at the real structural problems with our society.

In the 2019 elections the communal BJP, despite its failure to carry out its promises made in its 2014 poll manifesto, returned to power at the Centre with a huge majority. (It is small consolation that the party did not win any seat in Kerala where it had fielded candidates in all the twenty Lok Sabha constituencies.) The Left also fared quite badly. Against this background it is high time progressive and secular sections took the threat from the Far Right seriously and launch a united struggle against the canker of communalism, commodification of religion and demonstrable religiosity, besides pathologies like poverty, unemployment, diseases, oppression of dalits, adivasis and women, industrial and agricultural stagnation, and so on. In the present regime of neoliberalism, reactionary ideologies have become very profitable for those who hold the reins of power. At a time when the people of Kerala are emerging from the impact of the worst deluge of the century, there should be a collective effort to guard against modern-day Vamanas and Parashuramas turning this Mavelinadu, warts and all, into a neo-colonial Hindu rashtra and gifting it to greedy corporate brahmins.

REFERENCES

English

Aloysius, G. 2005. *Interpreting Kerala's Social Development.* New Delhi: Critical Quest.

Ambedkar, B.R. 2013. *Castes in India.* New Delhi: Critical Quest.

———. 2014. *Annihilation of Caste: The Annotated Critical Edition.* New Delhi: Navayana.

———. 2016. *Riddles in Hinduism: The Annotated Critical Selection.* New Delhi: Navayana.

Bhattacharji, Sukumari. 2002. *Myths: Vedic, Buddhist and Brahmanical.* Kolkata: Progressive Publishers.

Caldwell, Sarah. 2005. "Margins at the Center: Tracing Kali through Time, Space and, Culture." In *Encountering Kali: In the Margins, at the Center, in the West.* Edited by Rachel Fell McDermott, Jeffrey John Kripal. New Delhi: Motilal Banarsidass.

Chandramohan, P. 2016. "Developmental Modernity in Kerala." *Narayana Guru, SDNP Yogam and Social Reform.* New Delhi: Tulika Books.

Chandran, T.V. 2008. *Ritual as Ideology: Text and Context in Teyyam.* New Delhi: D.K. Printworld.

Deshpande, G.P. (ed.). 2002. *Selected Writings of Jotirao Phule.* New Delhi: Leftword Books.

Doniger, Wendy. 2009. *The Hindus: An Alternative History.* New Delhi: Penguin–Viking.

Islam, Shamsul. 2015. "Golwalkar: How The Breed Of Kerala Hindus Was Improved By Namboodiri Brahmins." *www.countercurrents.org.* 2 September. https://www.countercurrents.org/islam020915.htm. Accessed on 19 July 2019.

J, Devika. 2011. "Un-Indianizing Kerala: How to defend K K Shahina." *www.kafila.org.* 20 January. https://kafila.online/2011/01/20/un-indianizing-kerala-how-to-defend-k-k-shahina/. Accessed on 25 June 2019.

Jaiswal, Suvira. 2016. *The Making of Brahmin Hegemony*. New Delhi: Tulika Books.

Jeffrey, Robin. 1992. *Politics, Women and Well-Being: How Kerala Became a 'Model'*. New Delhi: Palgrave Macmillan.

Jha, D.N. 2004. "Looking for a Hindu Identity." Presidential address at Indian History Congress.

Joseph, Tony. 2019. *Early Indians: The Story Of Our Ancestors And Where We Came From*. New Delhi: Juggernaut Books.

Joshi, L.M. 2012. *Aspects of Buddhism in India*. New Delhi: Critical Quest.

Kapikkad, Sunny M. 2011. "Kerala Model: A Dalit Critique." In *No Alphabet in Sight: New Dalit Writing from South India*. Edited by K. Satyanarayana and Susie Tharu. New Delhi: Penguin.

Kochu K.K. 2011. "Writing the History of Kerala: Seeking A Dalit Space." In *No Alphabet in Sight: New Dalit Writing from South India*. Edited by K. Satyanarayana and Susie Tharu. New Delhi: Penguin.

Kosambi, D.D. 2008. *An Introduction to the Study of Indian History*. Bombay: Popular Prakashan.

Kumar, Aishwarya. 2018. "Were Women Allowed in Sabarimala? 25-Year-Old Affidavit by Travancore Devaswom Board Says Yes." *www.news18.com*. 12 October. https://www.news18.com/news/india/were-women-ever-allowed-in-sabarimala-debate-rages-on-amid-protests-by-true-believers-1907159.html. Accessed on 19 July 2018.

Kumar, Udaya. 2014. *"Dr Palpu's Petition Writings and Kerala's Pasts."* Paper delivered at Nehru Memorial Museum and Library.

Lennoy, Richard. 1971. *The Speaking Tree: A Study of Indian Culture and Society*. New York: Oxford University Press.

Mani, Braj Ranjan. 2015. *Debrahminising History: Dominance and Resistance in Indian Society*. New Delhi: Manohar Publishers.

Mani Vettam. 1975. *Puranic Encyclopedia*. New Delhi: Motilal Banarsidass.

Menon, Dileep. 2011. "Caste and Colonial Modernity." In *The Blindness of Insight.* New Delhi: Navayana.

Nair, Anita (ed). 2002. *Where the Rain is Born: Writings about Kerala.* New Delhi: Penguin.

Namboodiripad, E.M.S. 2006. quoted by Dilip Menon in "Being a Brahmin". In *The Blindness of Insight.* New Delhi: Navayana.

———. 2010. *History, Society and Land Relations: Selected Essays.* New Delhi: Leftword.

Nanda, Meera. 2009. *The God Market: How Globalization is Making India More Hindu.* Noida: Random House India.

Nath, Vijay. 2001. "From 'Brahmanism' to 'Hinduism'." *Social Scientist.* Vol 29, No 3/4. March–April. New Delhi: Tulika.

Naqvi, Saba. 2012. *In Good Faith: A Journey in Search of an Unknown India.* New Delhi: Rupa Publications.

Neelakantan, Anand. 2012. *Asura: Tale of the Vanquished.* Mumbai: Platinum Press.

Nehru, Jawaharlal. 1981/1947. *The Discovery of India.* New Delhi: Oxford University Press.

Omvedt, Gail. 2004. *Jotirao Phule and the Ideology of Social Revolution in India.* New Delhi: Critical Quest.

———. 2016. *Seeking Begumpura: The Social Vision of Anticaste Intellectuals.* New Delhi: Navayana.

Pampirikkunnu, Pradeepan. 2011. "Nationalism, Modernity, Keralaness: A Subaltern Critique." In *No Alphabet in Sight: New Dalit Writing from South India.* Edited by K. Satyanarayana and Susie Tharu. New Delhi: Penguin.

Panikkar, K.N. 2016. *Essays on the History and Society of Kerala.* Thiruvananthapuram: Kerala Council for Historical Research.

Patil, Sharad. 2012. "CPM's Kozhikode Congress cuts the Last Thread Connecting it to Tantriki Sruti's Tradition." in *Mainstream Weekly.* 16 June. http://www.mainstreamweekly.net/article3511.html. Accessed om 2 July 2019.

Ramachandran, T.K. and P.T. John. 2005. "The Sangh Parivar's initiatives in the Tribal Belt of Wynad in Kerala." In *Hindutva and*

Dalits. Edited by Anand Teltumbde. New Delhi: Samya.

Sanal Mohan, P. 2015. *Modernity of Slavery: Struggles Against Caste Inequality in Colonial Kerala*. New Delhi: Oxford University Press

Satchidanandan, K. 2011. "Representation of Social Reality in Art and Literature: Forms of Resistance with Special Reference to Malayalam Literature." In *Towards a New Horizon*. New Delhi: Janasamskriti.

Satyanarayana, K. and Susie Tharu (ed). 2011. *No Alphabet in Sight: New Dalit Writing from South India*. New Delhi: Penguin Books

Sen, Amartya. 2006. *The Argumentative Indian*. New Delhi: Penguin.

Sikand, Yoginder. 2003. *Sacred Spaces: Exploring Traditions of Shared Faith in India*. New Delhi: Penguin.

Sreedhara Menon, A. 2012. *A Survey of Kerala History*. Kottayam: D.C. Books.

Staal, Frits. 1961. *Nambudiri Veda Recitation*. The Hague: Mouton.

Thapar, Romila. 2014. "Syndicated Hinduism." *The Past as Present: Forging Contemporary Identities Through History*. New Delhi: Aleph.

———. *1996*. "The Tyranny of labels." *Social Scientist*. Vol 24, No 9/10. September–October. New Delhi: Tulika.

Veluthat, Kesavan. 2013. *Brahman Settlements in Kerala: Historical Studies*. New Delhi: Cosmo Books.

Viswanathan, S. 1999. "Deities of the People." *Frontline*. 9 April.

Malayalam

Baby, K.J. 1991)]. *Maveli Manram*. Thrissur: Current Books.

Frenz, Albrecht. 2001. "Report Regarding The Uprisings of the Mappilas in Gundert's Letters (Notes)." In *500 Varshathe Keralam—Chila Arivadayalangal*. Edited by V.J. Verghese. Thrissur: Current Books.

Gopalakrishnan, Naduvattom. 2003. *Kerala Charitradharakal*. Arayoor: Maluban.

Gopalakrishnan P.K. 1974. *Kerala Samskaracharitram*.

Thiruvananthapuram: State Institute of Languages.

Haridas, V.V. 2008. *Kshetram, Utsavam, Rashtreeyam.* Kozhikode: Poorna Publications.

Keezhallur, Latheesh. 2016. *Sree Mutthappan: Aithihyavum Charitravum.* Thrissur: Green Books.

Kometh, Rajesh. 2013. *Nattudaivangal Samsarichu Thudangumbol.* Thiruvananthapuram: Mathrubhumi.

Mohanavarma, K.L. 2006. "Onatthappa Kudavayara!" in *Onanilavu.* Edited by Latha Lakshmi. Kozhikode: Lipi Publications.

Narayanan, K. Aju. 2012. *Keralathile Buddhamathparamparyam Nattarivukalilude.* Thiruvananthapuram: National Book Stall.

Panikkassery, Velayudhan. 2008. *Kerala Charitram.* Kottayam: D.C. Books.

Pavanan, Rajendran C.P. 2008. *Baudhaswadheenam Keralathil.* Kozhikode: Kerala Bhasha Institute.

Peruvathur, Mukundan K. 1997. *"Onam Aruteth?" Avarnapaksha Rachanakal.* Ernakulam: Dooth Books.

Priyadarsanlal. 2006. "Vamanavatharathile Rashtratantram." *Kesari,* Annual Number.

Rajeev, V. 2015. *Aryadhinivesavum Namboodiri Samskaravum.* Thiruvananthapuram: National Book Stall.

Ranjit, P. 2011. *Malayaliyude Bhootakalangal: Onavum Samoohyabhavanalokavum.* Thrissur: Current Books.

Ravivarma, K.T. 2001. *Rigvedam muthal Onappattukal vare.* Kottayam: D.C. Books.

———. 2014. *Parashuraman: Oru Pathanam.* Thrissur: Kerala Sahitya Academy.

Sanu, M.K. 2013. *Dr P. Palpu Dharmabodhathil Jeevicha Karmayogi.* Thrissur: Green Books.

Sekhar, Ajay and Aju K. Narayanan 2012. "Buddhaprathimakale ippozhum Bhayakkunnathaarokke?" ("Who are Still Afraid of Buddha statues?"). *Mathrubhumi Weekly.* December 2–8.

Sreedevi, K.P. 2001. "Keralathile Namboodiri Sthreekalude

Gathakala Charithravum Varthamanavasthayum." In *500 Varshathe Keralam—Chila Arivadayalangal.* Edited by V.J. Verghese. Thrissur: Current Books.

Vallikkavu, Vijayan. 2009. "Adivasi Ayyappanum Eezhavathi Lalitayum." in *Jatibhedam, Mathadwesham.* Thrissur: Buddham Books.

Venugopala, T.R. 2017. *Sampathum Adhikaravum: Thrissuril Ninnulla Oru Kazhcha.* Thrissur: Current Books.

Verghese, V.J. (ed.). 2001. *500 Varshathe Keralam—Chila Arivadayalangal.* Thrissur: Current Books.

Acknowledgments

In writing this book I have relied on a vast variety of sources in English and Malayalam—books, articles in journals and magazines, public lectures, even letters to the editor—and have not necessarily been able to access primary documents. I am beholden to every one of the historians and scholars whose works helped me understand the issues under discussion, although I may have failed to mention all their names. For obvious reasons, I could not accept the views of everyone I consulted. Nor have I shied away from using my imagination when necessary. I had planned a more comprehensive work and wanted to go deeper into the subject. However, various exigencies of life did not permit this.

I must acknowledge the help I received from many persons in the writing and production of this work. First, I must thank the team at Navayana, publisher Anand and editor Alex, not only for bringing out the work of a first-time author like me but also for some necessary alterations. Despite their other preoccupations N.R. Levin and my son A. Sunil Dharan, both of whom teach in Delhi University colleges, went through the manuscript and suggested important changes. Discussions with them and others helped me correct some of the gross misconceptions I used to nurse. Besides, being nearly software-illiterate, I would panic when my laptop would develop some problem and Sunil would come to my rescue. Without his assistance I would not have been able to finish this work nor mail it to the publisher.

I owe thanks to Manu Pillai, Anand Neelakantan, Samhita Arni and Arshia Sattar for reading and endorsing my work at short notice.

Let me add that there is no intention to show any community or social or religious group in poor light: my only objective was to present a subaltern perspective on the appallingly iniquitous social order—economic, social and cultural—that mars life in a state which boasts of a high human development index. Nor is anyone other than the author responsible for any lapse or shortcoming that might have crept into this polemical work. I will be delighted if this slim book serves, even slightly, to loosen the vicious grip of fanaticism and religious intolerance on the Malayali mind.